FULLNESS OF HUMANITY:
CHRIST'S HUMANNESS AND OURS

T. E. POLLARD

THE FIFTIETH SERIES OF
CROALL LECTURES

The Croall Lectures, 1980

FULLNESS OF HUMANITY

Christ's Humanness and Ours

T. E. POLLARD

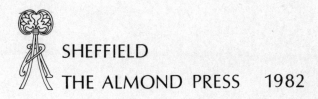

SHEFFIELD
THE ALMOND PRESS   1982

British Library Cataloguing in Publication Data:

Pollard, T. E.
   Fullness of humanity: Christ's humanness and
   ours.
   1. Jesus Christ - Humanity - Addresses,
   essays, lectures
   I. Title
   232'.8   BT218

   ISBN 0-907459-10-2
   ISBN 0-907459-11-0 Pbk

Published by
The Almond Press
P.O. Box 208
Sheffield S10 5DW
England

Printed in Great Britain
by Redwood Burn Limited
Trowbridge, Wiltshire
1982

Here one may

without much molestation

be thinking

what he is

whence he came

what he has done

and to what

the King has called him.

-John Bunyan

[Inscription on a tablet in
King's College Chapel, Aberdeen]

THE CROALL LECTURES, 1980

The Croall Lectures, Fiftieth Series, were delivered by Professor T. E. Pollard of Knox College, Dunedin, New Zealand, in the Martin Hall, New College, Edinburgh, 5th November - 20th December, 1980.

CONTENTS

PREFACE

The contents of this book were written primarily to be delivered publically as lectures. In presenting them for publication no attempt has been made to modify the lecturing style; they are presented as they were delivered except for minor changes at the end of Lecture I, and rewriting and expansion of the latter half of Lecture VI in order to develop further the discussion of "deification" in the Early Fathers.

Inevitably, given the nature of the undertaking, there are many loose ends in these Lectures. Loose ends, however, are not necessarily a fault, for they may stimulate hearers and readers to try to tie them up for themselves.

I must express my gratitude to the Croall Lectureship Trustees for the honour they have done me in inviting me to give the fiftieth series of Croall Lectures; to the Faculty of Divinity in New College in the University of Edinburgh, for its warm hospitality; to David and Margaret Gunn of The Almond Press for undertaking the publication of the Lectures; and by no means least to my wife, Noela, who carefully typed two recensions of the lectures.

Evan Pollard   Christmas, 1981
Knox College
DUNEDIN

7

Chapter I

INTRODUCTION: THE HUMAN PREDICAMENT

THERE is no more fundamental debate in the world today than that about human nature." Those were the words with which David Cairns opened his Kerr Lectures in Glasgow in 1949 on "The Image of God in Man."[1] There can be no doubt at all that this question remains fundamental and it appears always to have been so. The famous inscription at Delphi enjoined on those coming to consult the oracle: "Know thyself," and that dictum was to be the text on which Socrates based his philosophy. The Hebrew psalmist asked, "What is man?" (Ps 8:4), and Judaism sought to answer the question in terms of man's creation by God, and in the continuing story of the encounter of God with man and man with God in the history of his people.

In the Christian tradition the same question of the nature of man has been asked over and over again because of its central importance for the Church's faith in Jesus of Nazareth as the man in whom God has acted for us men and our salvation; that is, the question is of central importance for our understanding of the doctrine of the person and work of Jesus Christ. The question plays a fundamental role in the New Testament; the earliest heresy was one which either denied the reality of the humanness of Jesus, declaring it to be a mere appearance or phantasm (docetism), or reduced the significance of the humanness to no more than a burden which the divine Logos bore for a brief period, or a temporary garment worn by the Logos. Its importance was grasped by Church Fathers like Irenaeus, Tertullian and Hippolytus, as they tried to counter the bizarre speculations of the Gnostics, who themselves were confronting the same question, and by a Father like Athanasius, as he tried to

9

understand what it means to say that the Logos of God became man, and battled valiantly to prevent Christianity from compromising with polytheism and falling back into a pagan view of the nature both of God and of man. The question is central in the christological controversies of the fourth century and later: in Apollinarianism, Nestorianism, Eutycheanism, Monophysitism, Monotheletism and the rest.

Human nature became quite explicitly the subject of debate for Augustine as he wrestled with Pelagianism over the respective roles of grace and free will in the life of the individual human being, and for Anselm as he sought an answer to the question, "Why did God become Man?"[2] It was explicitly central in the writings of the early Italian humanists who pondered on "the misery of the human condition,"[3] and the nature and dignity of man: Petrarch, Pico della Mirandola, Manetti, and the others to whom Charles Trinkaus has re-introduced us in his magisterial work on the period[4] (even though Petrarch saw it from an odd perspective: he moved on from a discussion of "The Dignity of Man" to a chapter on remedies for toothache!).[5] The centrality of the question has remained in all humanist thought and in all Christian theology right down to our own day.

There should be no need to remind you of the debate over the nature and origin of man which followed the publication of Charles Darwin's "The Origin of Species" in 1859, and the consequent rise of the discipline of anthropology and its related disciplines of psychology and sociology, which seek to give a scientific account of the phenomenon of man. In the theological arena we have witnessed Karl Barth's reaction against the rather naive humanistic optimism of the old "liberal" theology of the late nineteenth and early twentieth centuries, epitomised in Adolf von Harnack's "What is Christianity?"[6] and the infighting in the neo-orthodox camp between Barth and Emil Brunner over the nature of man, the constitution of the "imago dei" and the effect which the Fall of Adam had on it. More recently we have seen the question of the nature of man at the centre of the various forms of existentialism, both Christian and secular. Its importance has been recognized by the World Council of Churches which, at Uppsala in 1968, established a Department of Humanum Studies, and by the Second Vatican Council, especially in the "Dogmatic Constitution of the

Church (Lumen Gentium)" and "The Pastoral Constitution on
the Church in the Modern World (Gaudium et Spes)"; the
latter asserts that "the pivotal point of Christian concern is
man himself, whole and entire, body and soul, heart and
conscience, mind and will,"[7] and talks freely about "the
birth of a new humanism."[8] It is significant, too, that the
first Encyclical of Pope John Paul II, "The Redeemer of Man
(Redemptor Hominis)" should also deal with this topic. He
speaks of "the human dimension of the mystery of
redemption," of the Gospel which "verifies every aspect of
authentic humanism" (10). He speaks of "man in the full truth
of his existence, of his personal being and also of his
community and social being" as "the primary route that the
Church must travel in fulfilling her mission" (14).

Now, however, it is possible to detect a shift in emphasis.
The primary concern is no longer the ontological or
existential question, "What is man?"; rather it is the
eschatological question, "What future is there for man?", or
perhaps in a form sharpened (or blunted?) by pessimism, "Is
there any future for man?", although, of course the questions
of the nature and destiny of man cannot be separated from
one another.

The First World War was declared to be "the war to end
war," and the aim of the Western Powers was "to build a
world fit for heroes to live in." During the Second World War
we heard a great deal about "the new world order" or "the
new social order" which would emerge once the Germans and
Japanese had been defeated, and we were told that we were
fighting for the Four Freedoms enunciated in "The Atlantic
Charter." In the euphoria of relief in the years immediately
following World War II, despite the horrors of total war,
despite the destruction of the Coventries and Dresdens and
Hiroshimas, and despite the still unimaginable ghastliness of
the Holocaust, we tended to take a pretty optimistic view of
human nature and the prospects for the future of mankind.
We looked forward to the better and braver new world we
were setting our hands to build, optimistic that we would be
capable of coping successfully with the many unresolved
problems still on the agenda. To be sure, there was a wide
variety of views of human nature, Christian, Humanist,
Freudian, Marxist, Existentialist; at that stage we scarcely
entertained the possibility that non-Christian religions
especially those of the East, might have views which should

be taken seriously. None of the views of human nature doubted that man had a future, and only Existentialism, at least in its Sartrean form, denied that man's nature and future had any meaning other than utter absurdity. (It is interesting to note in passing that the contemporary theology of hope seems to have been prompted to re-discover the dimension of hope by an atheistic Marxist philosopher).[9] At the same time we were all aware that the new technology, whose development had been accelerated by the wartime demand for more efficient production of ever more powerful, more effective, more devastating weaponry, had placed in human hands the means of instant destruction, not only for enemies but for the whole human race. Peace, in the sense of absence of global thermo-nuclear war, has been maintained on the basis of fear - the policy of the ultimate deterrent. But, as membership of the thermo-nuclear club has grown in numbers, the imminence of global destruction has increased and the possibility of an accidental pressing of the button has become more real. We now realize how naive our post-war optimism was.

Peaceful developments of technology are also placing question-marks over our human existence. Computerization is robbing us of our individual personal and private existence, reducing us to ciphers, just as previously industrialization with its production-lines turned human beings into parts of the machinery of mass-production. Automation now threatens the whole human race with redundancy, apart from the small handful of technocrats who push the buttons and watch the dials. Genetic manipulation or engineering opens the possibility of the unforeseen production of virulent cloned bacteria which, if allowed to escape from the test-tube, may be more disastrous than any of the great plagues of the past.[10] Nuclear technology, through human error, may produce a thousand Three Mile Bends and accidentally make large areas of the face of the earth uninhabitable. Increasing industrialization and the population explosion have spread over the world an increasing pollution of the environment. In 1945 the word "environment" was a technical term only in the psychological debate over which is the more determinative influence on man, heredity or environment. The word "ecology" was used only as a description of a branch of biological science, and according to the "The Concise Oxford Dictionary" (1942 edition) it was still being spelt "oecology."

Predictions of rapid population growth were treated with amused disbelief, yet figures released by the United Nations Organization in March this year tell us that in the past fifteen years the world's population has increased by 1,000,000,000, from 3,500,000,000 to 4,500,000,000 and the newscaster's comment was that it seems as though the human race is determined to breed itself to destruction. Already more than three quarters of the world's population lives a sub-human existence in sub-human conditions.

From the dawn of history, man has found the world, in which his lot is cast, to be a threatening one. The forces of nature were his enemies, enemies to be appeased or enemies to be overcome. Now, however, his lot is cast in a natural world which is threatened rather than threatening, and he himself, as part of the natural world, has become threatened man in a threatened world. Man himself, is becoming an endangered species. Furthermore, man himself, by his scientific knowledge and technological ability to harness, manipulate and utilize the resources of the earth and the forces of nature - man himself is responsible for the change that has taken place. The threat, of course, is also compounded by the completely natural human desire and determination of the hundreds of millions of men and women who are economically exploited and politically oppressed to liberate themselves from the powers that hold them in subjection. The countries of the Third World of Latin America, Africa and South East Asia have become human time-bombs. The desire for freeeedom - the four freedoms we spoke about so piously and so hopefully, the freedoms which we now assert to be basic human rights: freedom of speech, freedom of religion, freedom from hunger, freedom from fear - this natural desire for freedom is driving many, in desperation, towards violent revolution and terrorism which ultimately deprive their fellow human beings of the same basic rights and, indeed, even of life itself. On every side - and I have sketched in rough outline only a few of the factors - man finds himself threatened in a world that is threatened. And so the question about the meaning of life and of the possibility of a future for man becomes yet another question: "How can man be or become truly human in the face of the threat to his existence? How can man be what he ought to be, in the face of all the inhuman, antihuman, dehumanizing forces at work around him and within him?"

This predicament of late twentieth-century man, which daily grows more complex and hence more intractable, lays upon the Christian Church the prophetic responsibility now as always of proclaiming her message in ways which will speak God's word to the condition of humanity. It may be that some of the old language is no longer serviceable and that we have to find new ways of speaking. The attempt to do that will certainly bring upon us the accusation that we are altering the Gospel or departing from it, but every effort to translate the Gospel into new terms runs that risk. It was the awareness of the seriousness of this predicament and the awareness that the problem is expanding at an alarming rate that led to the crisis in the theology of mission in the sixties, which came to a head at the World Council of Churches Assembly at Uppsala in 1968 in the Section on "Renewal in Mission," with its emphasis on "humanization." The January, 1971, number of "International Review of Mission" was devoted to the subject "Humanization and Mission."[11] In his editorial, Philip Potter, asks "why humanization ... has become a major preoccupation of Christians," and after a brief indication of some of the factors which are dehumanizing man today, he says, "The question therefore is raised, with increasing agony: How can man be cured or at least curbed of his inhuman tendencies and actions and be enabled to be truly himself, an authentic person and at the disposal of his fellow-men for their mutual good?"[12]

Since Uppsala 1968 "humanization" has become a highly controversial issue in debate concerning world missionary strategy in relation to the two or three billion non-Christians; it is a clearly articulated implication of the theology of liberation; it has become a focal point in the debate on the doctrine of the person and work of Jesus Christ in the ever swelling flood of writing on Christology.

The emphasis on humanization has caused sharp antagonism, both at the theological level (of which that number of "International Review of Mission" is but one example) and at the practical level of opposing responses to the implementation of the policy of humanization (as the furore over the World Council's Programme to Combat Racism bears eloquent witness). This antagonism makes it appear that with the "discovery" of the word "humanization" something novel and unwarranted has been introduced into Christian faith and missionary strategy. Peter Beyerhaus for example has described it as "a radical shift of the centre from God to man, and accordingly the replacement of Theology by Anthropology ... a conscious turning away from God as the absolute and ultimate frame of reference for all Christian thinking and service."[13] Beyerhaus argues that in contemporary missionary strategy there is a radical polarization between salvation as traditionally understood and this new concept of humanization which emphasizes the need for the ameliorization of the conditions of human life if man is to be enabled to realise his full humanness. He says, "There is no bridge which leads us over from a social concept of humanization to the biblical mystery that by Christ's sacrifice we were not only vested with our true humanity according to his image, but made children of God and thus partakers of his divine life."[14] Thus he sharply opposes the individual and social dimensions of salvation, mission and humanization.

In the Uppsala Report, "Renewal in Mission,"[15] Beyerhaus sees a departure from what he aserts to be the biblical basis and aim of "mission" in the sense of "evangelization," which he would define in the supposedly traditional sense of "conversion of individual heathen"; the report, however, endeavours to keep in focus both dimensions, the individual and the social, as necessary for a proper understanding and fulfilment of the Church's task of mission in the name of Christ to the world today in its agonizing predicament. It is true, to be sure, that zeal for human rights, social and economic justice, freedom from exploitation and oppression, may lead to a man-centred ideology in which, to quote Beyerhaus again, "Even Jesus becomes just the prototype of an ideal social attitude, the 'man for others' whose resurrection and lordship mean hardly more than that the community of his followers is still inspired by his example."[16] It is equally true, however, that zeal for saving "souls" out of the darkness of this world may - and frequently does - lead to an otherwordliness which makes the individual so concentrate on the spiritual welfare of his own soul that he is oblivious to the injustice (unrighteousness) of the society around him and heedless of the cries of the oppressed. Overemphasis on the individual dimension of salvation may lead only too easily to a neurotic concern for self, to introspectiveness almost to the point of morbidity.[17]

In the first of his William Carey Lectures of 1970, M. M. Thomas gives a trenchant answer to Beyerhaus' criticisms of the World Council's emphasis on humanization. In reply to the argument that this involves "a radical shift from theology to anthropology," Thomas points out that "the ultimate framework of reference for Christian thought is neither God nor man in the abstract, neither the metaphysics of God nor the science of man taken in isolation, but Jesus Christ who is God-Man or rather God-for-Man, or to use Karl Barth's expresssion, the humanity of God. Therefore, properly speaking, Christian missionary thinking cannot be either theology or anthropology except as either of them is related to Christology. On the same reasoning, if it is Christ-centred, anthropology could become truly Christian in its framework. The distinction in humanism is between closed self-sufficiency and openness to the judgment and redemption of Christ in its spiritual inwardness."[18]

This is a point to which we shall have to return. It is sufficient to indicate that I believe that Beyerhaus' antithesis between theology and anthropology is a false one as also is the antithesis between individual and social (or corporate) salvation; both antitheses vitiate the truth of the Gospel of salvation as proclaimed in scripture and in the faith of the Church.

At the heart of the debate about humanization and the responsibility of the Church in relation to the social, political, economic, and racial problems which menace the lives of billions of our fellow human beings today, lies the question of liberation, particularly in those areas of the world where they are subjected to oppressive regimes which deny them their basic human rights. The proclamation by Jesus in both word and action of "good news to the poor, release to the captives, recovery of sight to the blind, liberation to those who are oppressed" (Luke 4:18; Isaiah 61:1), emphasizes the centrality of the message of liberation in Jesus' mission. We misunderstand and distort that message if we try to spiritualize it to mean simply the liberation of the human heart from sin. Certainly Jesus did not throw in his lot with the revolutionaries of his day and encourage terrorism; indeed there are some sayings which explicitly enjoin an attitude of non-violence. Nevertheless, in today's world, in which repression and oppression, injustice and unfreedom are imposed, if not in the name of religion or of a quasi-religious

ideology, at least with the active support or passive
acquiescence of the religious establishment, the question of
the legitimacy of the use of violence to achieve liberation
becomes a live issue. Despite our horror of violence, my
generation felt that it had to meet violence with violence in
order to resist the threat of totalitarian oppression. Who are
we to say to those actually living under oppression now, "You
must not resort to violence"? Our so-called Christian Western
world, for its own selfish economic and political ends,
hypocritically supports corrupt oppressive regimes in Africa,
Latin America and South East Asia and emotively brands as
"Marxists," "Leftists," "Communists," those who dare to
protest and cry out for freedom.[19] When millions of human
beings are treated as sub-human and are forced to live and
work in sub-human conditions, and yearn for liberation, it is
difficult to deny them the right to protest, violently if
necessary, aware though we may be that violence cannot be
the final answer, and the violent reaction against injustice
may very well result in a new regime in which injustice will
also be found.[20]

In the face of this situation today, is the Church to remain
silent to the cries of the oppressed, preaching a gospel of
individual salvation from individual sin but no gospel of
liberation from the corporate sin which is responsible for the
oppresssion of so many and preventing them from realising
their true humanity?

The impulse to humanization reaches out into another area
of our common human life to counter another threat to the
quality of human existence. Our exploitation of the resources
of the natural world and the correlative pollution of the air
we breathe, the water we drink and the food we eat, pose as
great a threat to the human race as any violent revolution or
global war. As John Reumann says:

All this new-found knowledge, technology, and
achievement, however, threaten to turn to ashes. We
attain new industrial goals, putting more cars on bigger
and better roads - only to discover we are disastrously
polluting the atmosphere and gobbling up the land with
strangling ribbons of concrete. We attain higher
standards of living - only to find the lake where we want
to go during new-found leisure time has become
contaminated and our civilization dying not merely in a

glut of "asphalt road and a thousand lost golf balls"[21] but in the refuse of our packaging, garbage, and trash. The ecology crisis of today scarcely needs to be detailed for anyone; it is upon us, in headlines and in a dozen daily annoying and sometimes potentially fatal ways.[22]

Here then is another area in which our humanity lies under the shadow of human self-inflicted dehumanization, and about this too the Church must speak.

When a number of theological issues become central at about the same time and are obviously interconnected, it is always very difficult to determine which issue has been the basic one of which the others are corollaries. Certainly the question of man's destiny or fate has been raised more and more acutely as the very progress which man is making technologically is placing him "under threat from what he produces," and raises the question "Is man, as man, developing and progressing, or is he regressing and being degraded in his humanity? Is man, as man, becoming truly better, that is to say more mature spiritually, more aware of the dignity of his humanity, more responsible, more open to others, especially the neediest and the weakest, and readier to give and to aid all?"[23] These are questions which the human predicament puts on the agenda of the world's discussion, questions being asked, not simply by Christians, but by secularist humanists, by Marxists, by Buddhists, Hindus, Muslims and all the rest.

Parallel with these questions imposed by the very predicament of man there has been a specifically Christian questing, directed at a deeper understanding of the centre and core of the Christian faith, namely, the meaning of the "incarnation" of God in Jesus Christ, not simply as an academic theological exercise (interesting though that may be) but also as the attempt to work out afresh the existential implications of the Christ-event for the life of the Christian in the world today and indeed for the life of the whole world. Whether it is the concern for the predicament of man that has forced christologians to return to a re-examination of the centre of the Christian faith in order to find a more secure place to stand in the fulfilment of the Church's prophetic role, or whether it is on the basis of a fresh understanding of "who Jesus Christ is for us today" that the christologians venture to enunciate the implications of christology for the task of the Christian and the Church in relation to the world - to try to decide which comes first is an idle exercise, because in every age there is interaction between the Church and the world, between theology and the dominant concerns of man; salvation history and secular history (if, after Pannenberg, such a distinction is still valid) overlap and interact. It is not that the Church allows the world to set the agenda. Rather the Church and her theologians try to proclaim the Christian message in a way which will best meet the deepest needs and longings of the world. Viewed in this way we have to acknowledge that the theological and kerygmatic expression of the Church's response to God's address to her is always culturally conditioned, and it cannot be otherwise if the Church is to proclaim God's word to every man in his own culturally conditioned situation. The study of church history and the history of dogma makes this crystal-clear, and it should hardly be necessary for examples to be produced. The early church sought to express its doctrine of salvation in terms of the victory of Christ over the principalities and powers; the mediaeval church was to express it in terms of Anselm's satisfaction theory which found its stimulus in the cultural and legal milieu of feudalism;[24] Luther expressed it in terms of justification by faith in reaction against the Roman Church's emphasis on the value of works in penitential discipline, and so on.

In our generation the focus of interest in christology has shifted to the real, authentic, genuine, full humanness of Jesus, an aspect of christology which the Church has always maintained but never clearly spelled out, and this concentration on the humanness of Jesus has coincided with the deep questioning of contemporary man and society about our human nature and the destiny of our human species at the time when our very survival is under threat. Attention is riveted on the man Jesus, whom the Church from the beginning has proclaimed to be the man in whom God has revealed himself for the salvation (liberation) of mankind. When we speak about "authentic" humanity, "real" humanity, "genuine" humanity, "full" humanity, as the goal of the human quest or the gift we seek from God, we are also saying something about how we understand the humanity of Jesus, and conversely, whenever we speak about the humanity of Jesus, we are also saying something about the humanity of man. Christology is not only thinking about Christ; it is also thinking about God and man,. For the Christian, theology and anthropology, as M. M. Thomas points out, are meaningful only as they are related to christology.

Hugh Anderson tells us that it is estimated that in the late eighteenth and nineteenth centuries over 60,000 lives of Jesus were published.[25] Now, in the latter part of the twentieth century, we are witnessing an outbreak of an epidemic of christologies, both at the scholarly and popular levels. It appears that suddenly a dormant virus of disenchantment with traditional christological formulations has become active, manifesting itself in a rash of books and articles. Some of them have quite sober and sedate titles such as, "Jesus the Christ,"[26] "Jesus - God and Man,"[27] "The Shape of Christology,"[28] through more arresting titles such as "Jesus Who Became Christ,"[29] "Jesus Christ Liberator,"[30] "Jesus: an Experiment in Christology,"[31] "Christology at the Crossroads,"[32] to even more startling titles such as "Jesus the Man and the Myth,"[33] "The Myth of God Incarnate,"[34] and to what are probably the ultimate ones, "Christologies: How up-to-date is Yours?"[35] and "Goodbye Chalcedon! Hello What?"[36] In all these christologies the problem of the humanness of Jesus occupies a central position, because it is recognized, possibly as never before, that it is through the humanness of Jesus that God has chosen to reveal himself and to reconcile the world to himself. This raises the question of the relationship of Jesus' humanness to our humanness. This shift in emphasis has, of course, been greeted with accusations from some directions that modern christologies are ignoring, or diminishing, if not actually denying the divinity of Jesus. I am trying, with the help of the Bible, Christian tradition and contemporary Christian thinkers to explore the meaning of "humanity," or "humanness," and to ask whether it is meaningful to speak of salvation as "humanization," and, if it is meaningful, to ask whether salvation, seen in this way, tells us anything at all about the humanness of Jesus, and therefore about us in our own present-day predicament. It may be impossible to reach an adequate understanding of Jesus' humanness apart from considering his relationship with God or apart from the presence of God with him or in him, but the same may be true also for our understanding of our humanness. It too can be understood only in the light of our relationship with God "in whom we live, and move, and have our being" (Acts 17:28). In focussing attention on "humanness," I am not leaving "divineness" out of account, I am not overlooking what at this stage I would prefer to call "the divine dimension" of Jesus. Ultimately our discussion of humanness will lead us to "the divine dimension."

Before proceeding any further, I should try to clarify why I choose the word "humanness" rather than "humanity." I may seem to be splitting hairs, but I want to try to avoid the ambiguity of the word "humanity," which may mean a universal (the whole human race) or an abstract quality. By "humanness" I seek to focus attention on what a man is or what he is intended to be. Further I want to avoid the overtones of the old christological dichotomy, the "humanity" and "divinity" of Jesus. In the light of my use of "humanness" in this sense, "humanization" then means the process by which a man is enabled to become what he is intended to be, that is, to be truly, fully, authentically human, either by an inward change within himself, or by an outward change of the circumstances in which his life is set, or by a combination of both inward and outward change.

I am aware that there is considerable debate as to whether the humanness of Jesus is the proper starting point for thinking about Jesus Christ (or indeed about man). Some contemporary christologians, for example Rahner, Küng, Sobrino, Boff, Schillebeeckx, Peter de Rosa, James Mackey, to mention a few, explicitly emphasize the humanness as the point of take-off for christological discussion, and think of their christologies as "christologies from below," as also do the contributors to "The Myth of God Incarnate." Moltmann sees this as a shift in emphasis which has taken place since the time of Lessing: "the vital question of humanity has for many become the main question about Christ,"[37] and he connects this concern, as they themselves do, with "the demand for true humanity, authentic life, inner identity and liberation."[38] Moltmann himself, however, wishes to make "the scandal and folly of the cross" "the basic problem and starting point of christology";[39] but for him the cross is to be seen not simply as the cross on which Jesus died, but rather "the cross of the Christ who is abandoned by God."[40] He is led to make the statement which is almost identical with Beyerhaus' protest against "humanization" mentioned earlier; Moltmann says:

Jesus is no longer understood against the background of discourse about God as "God-man," but as it were in the anthropological foreground as the exemplary and archetypal "man of God."[41]

Pannenberg, on the other hand, declares that the starting point is the resurrection, although I detect considerable inconsistency in his statements. He insists that "the method of a christology 'from above' is closed to us ... our starting point must lie in the question about the man Jesus,"[42] yet he proceeds to argue that "the relationship of Jesus to God must be discussed first, and only then can Jesus as man and as the fulfilment of human existence in general be discussed."[43] This leads him to discuss "Jesus' Resurrection as the Ground of His Unity with God,"[44] and "Jesus' Divinity in Relation to the Father's Divinity,"[45] before coming to discuss "Jesus the Man before God."[46]

With many others, Walter Kasper finds the starting point in "the confession of faith of the church community" that "Jesus is the Christ," but asserts that "its content and pre-given standard lie in the history and activity of Jesus."[47] Thus he takes up the insights of form criticism that all that the gospels tell us about the Jesus of history is mediated to us through the faith of the earliest Christian communities, and on that point all the contemporary christologians would agree with him. Most would also agree with him that there is a necessary connection and continuity between the Jesus of history and the Christ of faith.[48] Kasper's phrase "the confession of faith of the church community" is susceptible, however, of at least two interpretations. On first reading it seems to refer to the earliest church community, the immediate post-resurrection community, but it can also mean the church community within which we ourselves stand, and it is this latter meaning which seems to me to be the more adequate. The christological problem then, as Leonardo Boff, for example, points out so clearly,[49] is not simply the problem of the continuity of the Risen Lord acclaimed by the post-resurrection community in the writings of the New Testament with the Jesus of history, but the much larger problem of the relationship between the Christ we confess today as a church community, the Christ confessed in differing ways by different church communities in successive generations, the Christ confessed and acclaimed by the disciples after the resurrection, and the Jesus of history.

It is not my intention to formulate another systematic christology. In the remaining lectures I propose, rather, to sketch out how the Old Testament understands "humanness," how various strands of New Testament tradition see it, and then, in the light of this biblical understanding, to look at some of the things that have been said about humanness, Christ's and ours, by some of the Fathers and in some contemporary discussion. The journey ahead is rather perilous; at times we shall have to tread carefully, at others we shall have to make rather dangerous leaps. I myself am making the journey in the hope that in the end I shall understand a little more what becoming human and being human mean, both to God and to man, as we see our humanness refracted through the humanness of Jesus.

Chapter II

HUMANNESS IN THE OLD TESTAMENT

PERHAPS by a somewhat rambling route, I suggested in the first lecture that man's current predicament is that of an endangered species: endangered not simply as far as his existence is concerned, but also in that his very nature as man is threatened with increasing dehumanization. The emphasis on humanization in contemporary missionary strategy, paralleled by the emphasis on liberation in the theologies emanating from the Third World, is both a protest against dehumanization and an attempt to create a society or societies in which man may be enabled to find and express his true humanness.

In this response to the human predicament theologians have been driven to look afresh at christology, to ask what it means to say that Jesus was a man and how his being a man is related to the salvation, liberation, humanization of man today. The quest for a way through the human predicament leads us back therefore to Jesus of Nazareth; but we can only begin to understand Jesus and his impact as we see him against the background of the history and faith of the Jewish people among whom he came as the fulfiller of the promises of Yahweh. Let us turn, then in this lecture, to seek an understanding of how the religious tradition of the Old Testament, "the cradle in which Christ lies" as Luther put it, thinks of man.

The first feature that stands out in the Old Testament's view of man is that man has a history and is aware of having a history. This awareness involves man in ambiguity, in the tension between his being as an individual and his being-in-relationship. To be human means to live in relationship, in an I-Thou relationship with God, with his fellow man, and, equally importantly, although not so frequently recognized, in the I-We relationship of the individual with the community: family, clan, tribe, race. The Old Testament, through all its variety of literary genres, is the story of God's dealing with his people, Israel, of God redeeming his people, collectively and individually from all that oppresses them. The centre of Israel's faith is God's historical liberation of his people from Egypt's bondage. That liberating act was celebrated (and still is) each year in the Passover Festival, as Israel acclaims Yahweh as her deliverer and redeemer, saviour and liberator. This liberation Israel celebrates as a redeemed people, and the individual celebration of it is the individual's celebration with his people. Israel's "confession of faith" takes the form of recital of God's mighty, redeeming acts; Israel sings hymns of praise to God, acclaiming his merciful deliverance of "the fathers." The daily recital of the Shema (Deut.6:6ff) is enjoined on Israel lest "you forget Yahweh, who brought you out of Egypt, out of the house of bondage" (Deut 6:12). At the time of the offering of the first fruits the Israelite is commanded to confess his faith in what Kosuke Koyama calls "the Deuteronomic 'Apostles Creed' " which summarizes the whole theology of the Pentateuch."[1] There, as frequently elsewhere, there is a remarkable oscillation between singular and plural, "I" and "we," and at the same time the identification of the present generation (individual and corporate) with the past generations:

> A wandering Aramean was my father; and he went down into Egypt and sojourned there, few in number; and there he became a nation, great, mighty and populous. And the Egyptians treated us harshly, and afflicted us, and laid on us hard bondage. Then we cried to Yahweh the God of our fathers, and Yahweh heard our voice, and saw our affliction, our toil, and our oppression; and Yahweh brought us out of Egypt with a mighty hand and an outstretched arm, with great terror, with signs and wonders; and he brought us into this place and gave us this land, a land flowing with milk and honey. And behold, now I bring the first of the fruit of the ground, which you, O Yahweh, have given me (Deut 26:5-10).

Koyama comments that "this experience of emancipation from imprisonment - dead - alive - lost - found had decided the character of the biblical faith." Whether this is a genuine "confession of faith" or not, and whether, as von Rad held,[2] it is an ancient formula, or a Deuteronomistic creation, it is significant that it is the cultic response made by the worshipper as he offers the first fruits, and, as a cultic response, it consists of the recital of historical narrative,[3] in which the individual asserts his identity with both present and past generations of his people.

This theme of liberation from bondage, either of the individual or of the nation, is celebrated in psalms which specifically recall either the deliverance from Egypt or some other liberating action of God. There is the remarkable juxtaposition of Psalm 105, a majestic paean of praise to God in which Israel celebrates step by step how God delivered his people from Egypt, brought them through the wilderness and led them into the promised land, with Psalm 106, which is also a paean of praise, but recounts, not the mighty acts of Yahweh but the rebelliousness with which Israel responded to every move Yahweh made to liberate her.

This historical orientation of Israel's faith, both the faith of the community expressed in the cult and the faith of the individual expressed in personal piety, is emphasized clearly in the way in which Yahweh is continually referred to as "the God of our fathers," or "the God of Abraham, of Isaac, and of Jacob."[4] It is to be seen too in Israel's understanding of time. Hans Walter Wolff points out that for the Deuteronomist Israel's relationship with time "is different from the one familiar to us ... Man proceeds through time like a rower who moves with the future backwards: he reaches his goal by taking his bearing from what is visibly in from of him; it is in this revealed history that for him the Lord of the future is attested."[5] (It is interesting to note in passing that this same relationship with time is to be found among the New Zealand Maoris, who speak of the past being "in front of" them, or "before" them, and who have a deep sense of solidarity with the past of the tribe or race closely resembling that of Israel).

There has been among Old Testament scholars considerable difference of opinion concerning the idea of corporate personality and the relationship between it and the individual's self-awareness as an individual.[6] To be sure, it is impossible to deny that in the Old Testament man is seen in his individuality. Yahweh knows Moses by name (Ex 33:17);

27

Yahweh knows Jeremiah before he formed him in the womb (Jer 1:5); and the Psalmist can say, "In the Lord I take refuge" (11:1), "I love you, O Lord" (18:1), "The Lord is my shepherd" (23:1). "The Lord is my light and my salvation" (27:1), "I will lift up my eyes to the hills" (121:1). Further, "appreciation of man as an individual can be found in the names that are called 'theophoric names', i.e. those which are compounds of the name of God,"[7] names like Elijah, Elisha, Joel, Joshua, Jehonathan and many others. Martin Noth maintains that "personal names will always prove those wrong who maintain that they find in ancient times a relationship of divinity exclusively to the group."[8] Nevertheless, at the same time it cannot be denied that man appears primarily as an individual-in-community, that "the fate of the individual in Israel was largely the fate of his people,"[9] and at least in the pre-exilic period attention is concentrated on God's dealing with the group, or with the individual - judge, priest, prophet, king - as the representative of the group.

Albert Gelin argues that "the Hebrew mentality is so constituted that it likes to present in succession the variety of aspects of one single complete reality" and that "the 'individual-community' tension must be understood in the same way."[10] Thus he dismisses the view that there is a chronological development, an evolution from an early stage of corporate or community awareness of and response to God to a later stage of individual reponse. Against Gelin's view it can be argued that it is only in the developing prophetic tradition that the individualization of religion comes to explicit expression as an abstraction from the primary experience of the community before God. Wolff, for example, sees this happening in Jeremiah and being developed more fully in Ezekiel. "It is not the least of the Bible's contributions to anthropology that man should understand himself for the first time when he is an individual, summoned through the call of the imcomparable voice out of the bonds of his heritage and called to a new covenant."[11] Along with this we have to keep in mind the fact that in Judaism the destiny of man was bound up entirely with the destiny of the nation. The eschatological hope for the individual found expression only in the very latest stage of Old Testament development, with the idea of resurrection in Daniel 12:2 and Isaiah 26:19, and was further articulated and elaborated in the Inter-Testamental Literature, in II Maccabees 7,

Apocalypse of Baruch 30:2-5, and chapters 49-52, and elsewhere. Yet the individualization of the eschatological hope expressed in terms of bodily resurrection does not lessen the tension between individual and community. Individual resurrection is the individual's participation in the general resurrection at the last day (I Thess 4:13ff; I Cor 15) and in the New Testament it is expressed in terms of being "with Christ," "with the Lord," sharing in the Messianic banquet of which the Lord's Supper is an anticipation and foretaste.

Very closely linked with this historical orientation of Israel's faith, this awareness of personal and corporate interaction between Yahweh and Israel, is the idea of the covenant between them. Yahweh chooses, elects Abraham and his descendants to be his people. Initially the choice is expressed simply in terms of promise: "I will make you a great nation, and I will bless you ... and in you shall all the families of the earth be blessed" (Gen 12:2); "I will make your descendants as the dust of the earth" (Gen 13:16); but then the obverse side of the divine promise comes to expression in the establishment of the covenant with Abraham: "I am God Almighty; walk before me, and be blameless" (Gen 17) and circumcision is given as a sign of the covenant, the mark that distinguishes Israel as God's peculiar people.

The covenant is most simply expressed in the words, "I will be your God, and you shall be my people" (Lev 26:12; Jer 11:4, 30:32; Ezek 14:11 et al.). In fulfilment of his part in the covenant, God shows his steadfast love and faithfulness to Israel. His steadfast love (hesed) is manifested in his redemption of his people from bondage, and calls for Israel's response of "hesed" towards God, and for her expression of that "hesed" within her life as God's people. God's faithfulness (emet) in the covenant is his dependability: he is not a capricious God but one who is faithful to his promise, true to his word, and this too he has demonstrated in his saving activity in history in his leading of the patriarchs and above all in the liberation from slavery. Indeed the very making of a covenant is itself God's declaration of his steadfast love and faithfulness. The covenant with Abraham may be described as an "eternal covenant" (Gen 17:19), and yet, time and again, God renews his covenant, re-affirming his love and faithfulness in the face of Israel's rebelliousness and infidelity. This theme rings out clearly from the pre-exilic prophets like Hosea, and especially in Jeremiah's prophecy of the new covenant, which is set in the context of Yahweh's promise of restoration of the fortunes of his people who have just been carried off into exile (30:1-9), and his assurance of the everlasting nature of his love and the continuation of his faithfulness (31:1-3)[12] This new covenant (31:31ff) will be made with the house of Israel, yet it will bring in a new era in which the hearers of the word become individuals[13] and the individual in Israel "comes of age."

If the covenant which Yahweh establishes with Israel is the promise of his steadfast love and faithfulness, it also requires the responsibility of Israel, her response of faithfulness and love and her responsibility before Yahweh for her faithlessness and disobedience. Yahweh makes his demand explicit by giving the Law to Israel through Moses; "I the Lord your God am a jealous God, visiting the iniquity of the fathers upon the children to the third and fourth generations of those that hate me, but showing steadfast love to thousands of those who love me and keep my commandments" (Ex 20:5-6). By obedience to the Law Israel remains within the covenant. She is not saved by her obedience to the Law; she is not justified by works of the Law. By obedience, by works of the Law, by keeping her side of the covenant, she remains within the sphere of God's love and faithfulness, the object of God's redemptive dealing.[14] The Law is given so that Israel may be holy as Yahweh is holy (Lev 11:44; 19:1; 20:7): "you shall be holy, for I am holy." But the Law is not merely oriented towards Israel's relationship and responsibility to Yahweh, her partner in covenant. Yahweh's demand on Israel is not merely for right relationship with himself; it is also demand for right relationships within the community of his people. This is the burden of the pre-exilic prophetic call, the call for truth, honesty, justice, faithfulness, mercy. Amos castigates those in Israel who "sell the righteous for silver, and the needy for a pair of shoes" (Am 2:6), "who oppress the poor, who crush the needy" (4:1), who "trample upon the poor" (5:11), and calls Israel to "seek the Lord and live" (5:6), to "seek good, and not evil, that you may live" (5:14), to "let justice roll down like waters and righteousness like an overflowing stream" (5:24). Hosea recalls Israel to a faithfulness to Yahweh which will express itself in "steadfast love and not sacrifice" (Hos 6:6), and urges her, "sow for yourselves righteousness, reap the fruit of steadfast love" (10:12), "return to the Lord your God, for you have stumbled because of your iniquity" (14:1). Micah thunders against those who "covet fields, and seize them; and houses, and take them away; they oppress a man and his house, a man and his inheritance" (Mic 2:2), those "who abhor justice and pervert all equity" (3:9); and he asserts that what the Lord requires is "to do justice, and to love kindness, and to walk humbly with your God" (6:8). The double thrust of Israel's covenant responsibility is summed up by Jesus in his combining the two love-commands, "You shall love the Lord your God with all your heart" (Deut 6:5) "and your neighbour as yourself" (Lev 19:18).[15]

The covenant relationship, then, which is the primary fact of Israel's self-understanding, involves the I-Thou relationship of Israel with Yahweh her God, the I-We relationship of the individual Israelite with the community, Israel, and the I-Thou relationship of the individual Israelite with his fellow-Israelite and ultimately with his fellow-man, be he Israelite or non-Israelite.

Implicit in this historical orientation of Israel's faith, implicit in her awareness of being a covenant people bound to Yahweh by his love and mercy and compassion, implicit in her awareness of God's redemptive activity in and through the ups and downs of her history, implicit in her awareness of being under the Law which Yahweh has given - implicit in all this is the limitation of Israel's existence to life in this world and in this time. In a recent article on "Resurrection - Fact or Illusion?", Eduard Schweizer emphasizes the this-worldly orientation of Israel's life and expectations. "The Israel of the Old Testament experiences its God within this world and within the life on this earth ... Israel is living with its God on this earth, in the history of its time, in an existence which is time and again limited by birth and death."[16] Nevertheless, time-bound and space-bound though her faith in God and experience of God may be, Israel never places limits of time and space on God. He always stands over against his people as the one who is unlimited, indeed as the one who is the Lord of the limits, whom no man has seen or can see, the Lord, "high and lifted up," "sitting upon a throne" in whose presence the prophet can only cry, "Woe is me! For I am lost" (Is 6:1-5). He is the Lord who declares, "I am God and not man, the Holy One in your midst" (Hos 11:9); "I am Yahweh, that is my name; my glory I give to no other" (Is

42:8); "I am Yahweh, and beside me there is no saviour" (Is 43:11); "the first and the last" "beside whom there is no god" (Is 44:6). Yahweh is the absolutely incomparable one, present with Israel in her history, yet transcending history as its Lord.

The orientation of Israel's faith towards God as the Lord of history, who has acted in electing, leading and dealing lovingly and faithfully with Israel, led Israel to reflect on her own nature and condition as a people over against God, bound by space and time. The changing fortunes which befell Israel did not destroy her faith in the God of the covenant. To be sure, at times she may complain that God has forsaken her, yet she knows that it is she who has forsaken God; she has been faithless, rebellious, disobedient; she has fallen short of what God intends her to be. Her predicament in history makes her ask why these things should be? Why should the story of her relationship with Yahweh be such a tale of misery, such a series of rebellious acts, such a history of disobedience, unfaithfulness and defection from the covenant on Israel's part? These questions, which may be summed up in the one basic question of the origin of evil, the Yahwistic writer of the ninth or tenth century B.C. sought to answer with his story of the creation and fall of man in Genesis 2-11. Many Old Testament scholars emphasize that the two creation narratives of the beginning of Genesis have as their presupposition Israel's experience of Yahweh's creative act of redemption, when, out of the refugees fleeing from Egypt's bondage, Yahweh made them a nation, created them to be his people. "The creation accounts ... are written from the standpoint of the meaning disclosed in the event of the Exodus."[17] "From the Exodus Israel looked back to the creation, confessing that the God who was active at the beginning of her history was likewise active at the beginning of the world's history."[18]

So the Yahwist tells the story of God's creation of man to till the ground and of woman to be his helper and companion. God places limits on mankind by forbidding him to eat of the fruit of the tree in the midst of the garden, but man transgresses the limits, oversteps the mark, wanting "to be like God" (Gen 2:5), wanting to obliterate the distinction between himself and his creator. Thus for the Yahwist man is "defective man" (so C. Westermann).[19] The Yahwist was concerned "to point out the many ways in which man could fail,"[20] and in those sections of Genesis 2-11 which come from his hand we have the two groups of narratives in which we can see this happening. "In the one it is the individual who shows himself defective, either in relation to God (ch.3) or in relation to his fellow man (4:2-16); in the other it is mankind, the group, that is defective, once in transgressing the limits of race, and then in transgressing the limits of technology. In both cases the defect consists in overstepping man's limitations."[21] Westermann rightly draws attention to the unfortunate tendency of church tradition to isolate Genesis 1-3 and ignore chapters 4-11. "In the biblical accounts of the origins sin is not the narrow, individualistic notion that it has become in church tradition. It is viewed in a broader perspective. It is seen as that other limit, that inadequacy or overstepping of limits which determines the whole of human existence."[22] Yet it is significant that the Yahwist's insights into the origins of man and of man's sinfulness have left no mark on the rest of the Old Testament, and it is only in late Jewish tradition (IV Esdras, for example) that his insights are developed and we find the beginnings of the typology of Adam which Paul was to develop in his christology and soteriology.

Attention is frequently drawn to the very wide differences between the Yahwistic and Priestly accounts of creation in Genesis 2-3 and Genesis 1 respectively, based as they are on divergent premises and expressed as they are in differing narrative forms. Yet, as Wolff points out, the two accounts agree in three essential points: (a) man belongs in immediate proximity to the animals; (b) through the special attention God devotes to him, man is at the same time unmistakably differentiated from the animals; and (c) it is only man and woman together who make up a whole and useful person.[23] But the contrast is of still greater importance. The Yahwist's account has man being evicted from the garden and continuing, in the world beyond the garden, the disobedience which has caused his eviction. The Priestly account, on the other hand, which finds echoes elsewhere in the Old Testament (e.g. in Psalm 8, Job 7:17-18; Ps 144:3-4; and frequently in Deutero-Isaiah), has no word about the misery of man; rather it emphasizes the dignity of man, who is created by God "in our image, after our likeness" (Gen 1:26), who is blessed by God: "Be fruitful and multiply, and fill the earth and subdue it" (1:28), to whom God gives dominion over all created things (1:29-30). And it ends with God's satisfaction with the goodness of all that he has made, and resting from his labours on the seventh day. One of the greatest puzzles of the Old Testament for me is why the earlier Yahwistic account, which gives a rationale for the ups and downs of Israel's history, should appear to have left so little impression on the rest of the Old Testament, while the Priestly account which speaks of a dignity belonging to man finds such frequent echoes.

In the Yahwist's account man is created for a paradisaical existence, an existence marked by what may be called an innocent dignity which he loses by his disobedience. In the Priestly account man is made in the image of God and given the dignity and responsibility of subduing the earth and having dominion over all creation. It is possible that the Priestly account, though later, was placed first in order to give the greater emphasis to this dignity and responsibility of man which persists through all the follies and sins of man in his journey through history? Is it that the Priestly writer is saying, "This is what God intends man to be; this is what it means to be human. This is the ultimate destiny of man. His sinfulness and rebelliousness will ultimately be overcome and man will become again what God made him to be"?

Is this, however to do justice to the Priestly writer's witness that man is made in God's image and after his likeness, the theme which is taken up in the New Testament and plays such a vast role in the development of christology in the early church and in the doctrine of man and sin particularly in the churches of the Reformation? In succeeding lectures we shall have to pay some attention to that theme, but here I am not concerned to argue about the meaning of the concept for the Old Testament author or about whether the image was lost or only defaced. It seems to me that what was originally a metaphor used to emphasize the dominion over nature which God has given to man, as his representative, has been made the basis for dogmas to which it has little real relationship. James Barr suggests that the function of the term "image of God" is to place man in a special or peculiar relation with God; if it were absent from the structure of Genesis 1, he says, the effect would be that man was only a dominant animal.[24] The same point is made in a recent note by Norman Snaith who says that "both Gen 1:26 and Ps 8 say that God made man to be his regent on the earth: man was intended (made) to rule all created things for

God." Snaith goes on to say, "The tragedy of this world is that as man has developed (<u>alias</u> 'become civilized'), more and more he has exploited the world and everything and every living creature that is in it: including his fellow man, at home and abroad, and especially those fellow men of his who are less 'civilized' than he is."[25]

It may well be that the truth of the human condition is to be found in the older, more primitive, more mythical narrative of Genesis 2 and 3 in which the author foresees the predicament of "man who would himself be dominated by the potentialites of the creation which he himself was designed to dominate." As Hans Walter Wolff says, "Wherever man is overpowered by the thing which he himself is meant to overpower, inhuman man is born."[26]

In the period (exilic or early post-exilic?), when the Pentateuch was taking its final shape, and the early history of Israel and her liberation from Egypt were being placed within the cosmological (or "ktisiological") framework of God's creative activity, and with the increasing emphasis on the individual, Israel appears to have become more conscious of the transcendence of God. Second Isaiah had stressed "creation-faith in a way no previous prophetic figure ever had,"[27] possibly, indeed almost certainly, in reaction against the creation-myths which the exiles had encountered in Babylon, which the exiles saw being re-enacted in the great annual festival processions, "when Marduk was enthroned as King and the chaos-battle ritually re-enacted."[28] The Priestly account of creation in Genesis and the Deutero-Isaianic expressions of creation-faith belong within the same life-setting, and represent an Israelite demythologization of the pagan creation-myths and the formation of what Carl von Weizsäcker, in his Gifford Lectures of 1959-60, so aptly calls "the anti-mythical myth."[29] Israel never allows history to become subordinate to nature; although she may believe her God to be "the Creator of the ends of the earth" (Is 40:28), she never allows God to be pushed out into unhistorical or a-historical transcendence. The Creator-God never ceases to be the God of Abraham, of Isaac, of Jacob. Ronald Gregor Smith made this point clearly in his lectures given in Melbourne and Dunedin in 1955, published under the title, "The New Man":[30]

In the context of the Bible we find a remarkable

conjunction of belief in a transcendent God with the significance of the actual history of the people of Israel. The transcendence is not acquired or possessed by Israel as an addendum to this history, it is not excogitated from the events in such a way as to leave the events behind; nor is it imposed upon the events in such a way as to exalt the transcendence at the expense of the reality of the events. But the two are woven together in an inextricable web which is itself the one single reality for Israel. Their history is their relation with God; and God is their history. Even in the highest flights of the psalmists and the prophets the holy and majestic Creator is all the time the one who is known by his mighty acts towards and with and in the life of Israel.

That is to say, Israel's creation-faith had as its presupposition her redemption-faith which had been forged in the burning heat of her experience of liberation by God from slavery and wilderness wanderings and of God's continuing mighty acts for her redemption. Indeed, if creation-faith arose out of her faith in the God who, by redeeming her, had created her as his people, Israel, then the primary purpose of Deutero-Isaiah's amazing use of creation language is "to get across a message of redemption";[31] and, as John Reumann points out, this leads on naturally to the expression of Israel's hope of future redemption in terms of "new creation," an idea not explicitly used by Deutero-Isaiah, but coming to explicit expression in the unknown prophet's equally unknown successor in Trito-Isaiah:[32]

Behold, I create new heavens and a new earth ...
Behold, I create Jerusalem a rejoicing,
    and her people a joy (Is 65:17-18)

The pre-exilic prophecy of the new covenant (Jer 31:31) thus becomes the prophecy of a new creation, a new created order or a renewed created order, as the scenario for the continued (and continuing) history of God's people as the people of the new covenant. This new creation is described in very this-worldly terms of the fulfilment of Israel's nationalistic hopes, with "the nations" flocking to Jerusalem with their gifts to do homage to Yahweh and to submit to Israel's sovereignty. In this sense the "eschatology" of the Old Testament is hardly a doctrine of "the End"; it is rather a doctrine of the ultimate situation which will be established on earth, albeit on a new or renewed earth. Israel will find her fulfilment as God's chosen, covenant people in history; presumably the individual qua individual will also find his fulfilment, his fullness of life, his fullness of humanity within the community of God's people within the eternal covenant. The end-time will be as the beginning-time. New creation, re-creation, is the redemption of Israel, the renewal of the cosmos, even the redemption, the liberation, the human-ization of mankind.

It is necessary to look finally and briefly at two developments in late pre-christian Judaism, namely the development of apocalyptic literature on the one hand, and of the wisdom literature on the other. Both of these de-velopments are so variegated in pattern that it is possible here to make only brief generalizations. Apocalyptic is the further development of Israel's hope for redemption, renewal, re-creation, necessitated by the apparent (and quite evident!) inability of man (or Israel) to achieve the quality of life which God intends him to have, for which God creates and redeems him. In the face of oppression and constant harassment, when the situation becomes desperate, the pendulum swings towards the idea that only God can put things right, and that he will intervene in a spectacular way to establish righteousness on earth. There is an "apocalyptic" element in all Old Testament prophecy, but it is when the lamp of hope burns low and dark despair sets in that apocalyptic comes into its own. "Hope rests not in human achievement but solely on what God will do by his miraculous intervention."[33] Yet still the picture, unworldly though much of the apocalyptic detail may be, is that of a continuing history on a continuing, though renewed earth - a continuing history, if not for all men, if not for all Israel, at least for the faithful remnant and for the faithful individual. In the late apocalypse of Isaiah 24-27 and in the Book of Daniel, for the first time "the eschatology of the individual" comes to clear expression making what Oliver Rankin called "a hesitating appearance." The idea of resurrection of the dead, "some to everlasting life, and some to shame and everlasting contempt" (Dan 12:2) implies, for the righteous, a liberation, renewal of life and a continuing historical existence. This too is implied in the vision of the "one like a son of man, the people of the saints of the Most High" (Dan 7:9-27), to whom "the everlasting Kingdom" will be given, and whom "all dominions shall serve and obey" (Dan 7:14 and 27). Amidst all the bizarreness of apocalyptic imagery, there is an earthy this-worldliness which becomes more so in the intertestamental apocalypses with the explicitly physical concept of resurrection of the body, for example, in the Apocalypse of Baruch, 49-52; "The earth shall then assuredly restore the dead ... it shall make no change in their form but as it has received, so shall it restore them" (50:2).

It is an interesting phenomenon that at the very time when Jewish apocalypticism came to full flower, with its emphasis on the divine intervention to bring liberation from oppression and fulfilment of life to Israel or the righeous within Israel, there should also come to flower another development of Jewish literature which appears to put all the emphasis on human effort and places the individual human being at the centre. How prophetic, apocalyptic, and wisdom literature are related need not concern us here, except to note that contradictory though they appear to be at many points, they stand side by side, and frequently are interwoven. Apocalyptic and wisdom are interwoven in Daniel and I Esdras, while Wisdom of Solomon 1-10 may be seen as a commentary or midrash on the Servant Songs of II Isaiah.[34] At about the same time as the idea of resurrection of the body makes its hesitating appearance, so also does the idea of immortality of the soul, the former "infiltrating into" or "percolating through" from Persian thought, and the latter apparently seeping in from Greek thought. I say "apparently" because I think a good case can be made that the immortality passages in the Wisdom Literature, in particular the Wisdom of Solomon, are to be seen as the attempt to express resurrection-belief in terms that Greeks could understand rather than as the substitution of a Greek belief for a Jewish belief.

All three strands of the Old Testament thought were concerned with man, with man in history, with man in relation to God. The different attitudes which appear contradictory may also be seen as complementary. Through the prophets God declares his message to man, sets out to meet man and find him in all the ambiguity and tension of his existence in community, and of his individuality. In apocalypticism God proclaims the imminence of his intervention in history to transform history, to resolve the ambiguity and tension of human existence, and to establish the perfect environment in which man (usually restricted to Israel or the righteous few in Israel) can find his true humanity in relation to God. "In wisdom, however," as von Rad says, "man was in search of himself and took things into his own hands ... He strove to discover his humanity in the sphere which had been allotted to him by God."[35] Wisdom, he says, was "Israel's attempt to unfold her humanity,"[36] the culmination of a process of "humanization" in Israel's thought which grew out of the demythologization of the surrounding nature religions, out of the disintegration of what Martin Buber felicitously called "pan-sacralism."[37] Israel only knew man as "a related man, related to other men, to his environment, and not least to God."[38] Von Rad points out that if man is to be able to live at all and make something of his life, he needs "room to manoeuvre." Wisdom taught Israel that despite natural catastrophes, life in the world is determined by "orders in which man could feel secure"; therefore "man's humanity was threatened all the more by man himself, by his own lack of order and his own folly ... all that lacked order, and all that destroyed life emanated from man himself."[39]

Thus, at the close of the pre-christian era, Judaism manifested itself and its view of man and history in a multiplicity of ways, impossible to harmonize into a consistent picture, yet each contributing something to the variety of thought we shall find in the New Testament and in the continuing tradition of the Church. All of them think, not of man per se, not of man qua individual, but man in relationship. The basic contribution of Jewish anthropology is the "relationality" of man.[40]

Chapter III

JESUS AND HUMANNESS IN THE SYNOPTIC GOSPELS

IN THIS lecture I want to concentrate attention on the witness of the synoptic Gospels, realizing only too well the problematical nature of the material with which we have to deal and the fact that nearly every inch of the ground to be covered has been, or still is, a battleground strewn with the debris of scholarly skirmishes. If we are to discuss humanity, humanness, and humanization in the New Testament, however, it is impossible to see how we can start from anywhere other than from the Jesus of Nazareth, whom the Gospels depict as a man, as a Palestinian Jew, whose history can be both located and dated. We must acknowledge that this Jesus of the Gospels is refracted through the resurrection-faith of the earliest followers, that the Gospels are kerygmatic rather than biographical, that the Jesus-tradition was both coloured by the earliest Christians' awareness of the presence and power of the risen Lord and adapted to meet the needs of the developing Christian communities in evangelization, liturgy, catechetical instruction and so on. Yet, having admitted all that, and recognizing the meagreness of verifiable historical detail available, nonetheless we cannot escape the fact that a recognizable human being steps forth from the pages of the Gospels to meet us as we read, baffling, mysterious, ultimately inexplicable though he may be. Despite all his scepticism about the possibility of knowing anything certain about Jesus' life and personality, Bultmann could still declare that "we know enough about his message to make for ourselves a consistent picture."[1] Bultmann's reaction against the psychologization that marked the old lives of Jesus has carried over into the new quest with the refusal to entertain the possibility of knowledge of Jesus' psychological development, or of his self-consciousness.

Many have protested against the extreme scepticism that has marked so much Jesus-research in this century, among them, by no means least, Hugh Anderson, to whose book, "Jesus and Christian Origins," I am greatly indebted.[2] With good reason, Anderson hesitates "to probe into his consciousness on the basis of the titles applied to him in the Gospels" and prefers "to dwell on his eschatological message as a possible clue to his 'Christological' claim upon men."[3] Fascinating though title-research is, the uncertainty surrounding the question whether Jesus himself used the "titles", and, if he did, what meaning the titles had for him, makes the attempt to get at Jesus' self-consciousness through the "titles" a rather tentative and hazardous enterprise. To give one brief example, "the apocalyptic Son of Man" makes his exits and his entrances in learned journals, but there are no signs that the problem of the Son of Man title is any nearer to being solved and it may be that the safest conclusion is to resign ourselves to the likelihood that it may remain insoluble.

It is not my intention to go into details about individual sayings or deeds of Jesus recorded in the Gospels. Rather I wish to come at this question of Jesus' self-consciousness by another route. We have already emphasized that the Old Testament sees Israel and the individual Jew as existing in history and as finding its humanness in relationship at all levels of life. This concept of relationality has, of course, been made familiar to us through the religious philosophy of Martin Buber, but as far as I am aware, it has had little effect on study of the Gospels in particular and of the New Testament as a whole. To be sure, there are links between Buber's relational personalism and the existentialism of Bultmann and his pupils, but the latter have placed undue emphasis on the individual, possibly as a legacy from Kierkegaard's discovery of "the individual" in the nineteenth century. It is among Roman Catholic exegetes and theologians, it seems, that the idea of relationality has been taken most seriously in the study of christology and of what it means to be human, and it is by them that the most stimulating advances are being made.

In an essay entitled "Current Problems in Christology," first published in German in 1954,[4] Karl Rahner launched a protest against the selective exegetical use of the Bible in supporting classical and scholastic christology which, he said,

> contrives to get along with a handful of texts from the Bible. Its predetermined goal is the dogma of Ephesus and Chalcedon and nothing more. The only texts from Scripture ... in which it is interested are those which can be translated as directly as possible into the terms of classical metaphysical christology. The method is a legitimate one; but it cannot cover the whole ground. A whole body of christological statements remains unused in this way, statements which describe Jesus' relationship to the Father (God) in the categories proper to conscious experience (existentially): Jesus as the only one to know the Father, Jesus who brings tidings of him, does his will at all times, is always heard by him and so on. The question, then, is whether it is possible on this basis to construct a christology in terms of Christ's consciousness.[5]

This article by Rahner has become programmatic for Roman Catholic christological thinking, and it may well be that it can help us to find a route through to a better understanding of the humanness of Jesus and its relationship to our humanness. Some fifteen years or more after Rahner's protest against the selectivity of classical-scholastic christology in its use of "a handful of texts from the Bible," Maurice Wiles, in a now famous and much re-printed essay, "Does Christology rest on a Mistake?",[6] made a similar protest, against the early church's use of a few passages, while ignoring or misinterpreting other New Testament passages which could have led the church to a considerably different christology. Whether Wiles would think of "Christ's consciousness" as a basis for christology is another matter. It is significant that it is systematic theologians who are insisting on raising the question which New Testament scholars have been trying to side-step. John McIntyre refers with approval to Leonard Hodgson's "now famous remark ... that the question of the knowledge of the incarnate Lord is the major christological issue of recent times."[7] This question has been taken up by most recent Catholic christologians (e.g. Küng, Schillebeeckx, Sobrino, Mackey and others).

We return to the synoptic Gospels. They nowhere argue

about whether Jesus was human or not (or whether he was divine or not). They do not present us with a clearly worked-out christology or anthropology. They present us with a "recital" of the deeds and words of Jesus of Nazareth within and as part of human history, a narrative in which the man, Jesus of Nazareth, encounters men and women amidst all the tensions of their daily existence, proclaims to them in word and deed the reality of God's kingly power and presence which is in the process of being realized in their midst both as judgment and gracious liberation. He proclaims God's providential care over all his creatures and his fatherly love towards all mankind. Through the "recital" of his words and deeds, they show us Jesus in relation to God, in relation to the task God has given him, in relation to his fellow-men, both those whose side he takes and whose cause he makes his own, and those who stand against him. He transcends all the traditional attitudes of what Hans Küng calls "the Jewish quadrilateral,"[8] aligning himself neither with the ecclesiastical and political establishment (the Sadducees and High Priestly family), nor with the revolutionaries (the Zealots, the first-century P.L.O), nor with those who had opted out of society to form a commune with an alternative life-style (the Essenes of the Dead Sea Sect), nor with moral compromisers who interpreted the Law to suit their own ends, taking it literally but giving the letter "an elastic interpretation" (the Scribes and the Pharisees).[9] Instead, he throws in his lot with the outcasts and no-hopers, "the sinners" (or as William Barclay translated "hamartolöi," "those with whom no respectable Jew would have anything to do"[10]), and the socially unacceptable tax-collectors. He identified himself with the common, ordinary folk who suffered from oppression and poverty in a corrupt society which received the sanction and support of the ecclesiastical establishment. To put it into traditional terms he identified himself with sinners and symbolically acted out this self-identification with sinners at the beginning of his ministry when he submitted to "baptism of repentance for the forgiveness of sins" (Mk 1:4) at the hands of John the Baptist. This theme of self-identification with sinners is developed in the New Testament in the enunciation of the christology of humiliation and exaltation, and of the doctrine of the atonement.[11] The Saducean establishment comes to see his apparently harmless activity as politically subversive; the

Zealots would have seen him as a rather harmless pietist who was making religion "the opiate of the people"; the Pharisees saw him as one who was usurping their religious authority, which they believed had behind it the authority of God and his Torah; the Essenes, of whom the Gospels make no mention, would have seen him as compromising with the evil world from which they had withdrawn entirely in order to keep themselves pure and spotless for the day of Messiah's coming.

This activity of standing beside the helpless and defeated, the alienated and troubled, this identification of himself with his fellow human beings, which in itself is a protest against the attitudes of those who opposed him, gives us some insight into Jesus' self-consciousness; he consciously sees his mission in terms of coming "to seek out and save those who are lost" (Lk 19:10), in terms of making present through his actions as well as through his words the sovereign rule of God who reigns not only as king but also as Father. This point is emphasized by Hugh Anderson when he asks what he calls "the stubborn question," "How were those who encountered him in the days of his flesh brought into the presence of the transcendent God?", and answers that "it was something in the person of Jesus, in his gestures, his deeds, his 'loving conduct', culminating in his Passion and death on the Cross, that gave his words their unique urgency and potency and eschatological cutting edge."[12] He goes on to say that, "in view of the historical sources, ... in regard to Jesus, word and deed, deed and word were inseparably allied."[13] Both his words and his deeds reveal that Jesus was conscious of being "a man with a mission."

This mission, described in Luke 4:18-19 in terms of being anointed by the Spirit of the Lord "to preach good news to the poor," and being sent "to proclaim release to the captives" and so on, and "to proclaim the acceptable year of the Lord," is a God-given prophetic mission, a sending, described, of course, in the words of Isaiah 61, and accepted and affirmed with the brief comment, "today this scripture has been fulfilled in your hearing" (Lk 4:21). It is the mission similarly described in words drawn from Isaiah 35:5-6 and 61:1 in answer to John's question, "Are you he who is to come, or shall we look for another?" (Mt 11:5). It is interesting, in passing, to compare these two incidents. Jesus' reading in the Nazareth synagogue is found only in Luke, and for that reason is suspected by some as a construction by the early church rather than authentic Jesus-tradition. Yet the sequel, leading through initial pleasure and wonder at Jesus' "gracious words" to the challenge, "no prophet is acceptable (dektos) in his own country" (v.24), then to the wrath of the hearers and their attempt to lynch Jesus, corresponds closely to the incident of John's disciples (which is Q-tradition), which leads up to the challenge, "Blessed is he who takes no offence at me" (Mt 11:6; Lk 7:23). That is, "Blessed is he who is prepared to accept me and my words." James A. Sanders has drawn attention to the link in Luke 4 between "the acceptable (dektos) year of the Lord" (v.19) and "no prophet is acceptable (dektos) in his own country" (v.24). In this latter Luke has "acceptable" in place of "not without honour" in Matthew (13:57) and Mark (6:4), and Sanders argues that Luke's use of "acceptable," rather than Matthew and Mark's "not without honour" is true to the original setting.[14] Be that as it may, there is no reason to doubt that Jesus was conscious of having been sent by God, having a mission on behalf of God to bring to men in word and deed the good news of God's forgiving love and fatherly care.

Although, as we shall see in a later lecture, John's Gospel heightens the emphasis on Jesus' awareness that he has been "sent" by God, "come" from God, "given" by God, the idea is by no means absent from the Synoptics (see Mk 9:37 = Mt 10:40 = Lk 9:48; Mt 21:37 = Mk 12:4), although even within the Synoptics themselves it is possible also to detect a heightening of the emphasis already at work. For example, compare Mk 1:38 with Lk 4:43. The setting is the same, but whereas in Mark Jesus says, "Let us go on to the next towns, that I may preach there also; for that is why I came out," in Luke Jesus says, "I must (dei) preach the good news of the Kingdom of God to the other cities also; for I was sent for this purpose." Luke changes the permissive "may" to the "must" of divine necessity, and the "came out" to the stronger "was sent." Yet the sense of mission is there even in the weaker Markan form, and elsewhere in Mark we find the divine "must," particularly in the predictions of the passion. In the latter, while the hand of the redactor may be present, I do not doubt, as I have argued elsewhere, that Jesus gave expression to the possibility, indeed the certainty, with which he foresaw that his mission would end in a violent death.[15] José Comblin puts it very strongly thus: "After a rapid entrance upon his ministry and the enthusiasm of some months over the signs he gave the seed was sown. Thereafter, all of Jesus' preoccupation was directed to his unavoidable death ... Jesus foresaw his death as part, in fact, as the principal part, of his mission ... of course, we perceive the hand of an author who narrates events after they have happened. However, the theme of the continual preoccupation of Jesus with his coming death is still there."[16] Or, as Hans Küng puts it even more bluntly, "No supernatural knowledge was required to recognise the danger of a violent end, only a sober view of reality ... Jesus' death was the penalty he had to pay for his life."[17]

This picture of Jesus' carrying out his mission necessarily implies two other aspects of his personality, neither of which finds much explicit expression in the Synoptics but which are nonetheless there. They are Jesus's absolute obedience to God and his faith in God. For some reason neither of these has played much part in discussions of the Jesus of the Gospels until quite recently. Here we shall concentrate on the obedience, reserving the discussion of the faith of Jesus until a later lecture. Scholars frequently make passing references to Jesus' obedience but seldom linger to investigate its implications for our understanding of the humanness of Jesus. "What strikes us about the Gospel story is that, as a man among men, Jesus claims nothing for himself as a man," says Anderson, "but everything for the God and Father, to whom he is utterly obedient and on whom he is utterly dependent."[18] Jesus, in his ministry, makes God's cause in the world his cause,[19] and gives himself entirely to it. Or, to quote Pannenberg, "The earthly Jesus lived in obedience to his mission totally in dependence upon the Father and in dedication to him."[20] The Reformers may have drawn a distinction between Jesus' active and passive obedience[21] but, in his total dedication to his mission, active and passive become one. The divine necessity, the Father's will, becomes the active obedience of Jesus. Usually discussion about Jesus' obedience occurs in connection with his death, and that in relation to the hymn in Philippians: "he humbled himself and became obedient unto death, even death on a cross" (Phil 2:8). That surely implies, however, that as a man ("being found in human form") he was utterly obedient, and that his voluntary acceptance of the ignominious death on a cross demonstrated just how total his obedience was. Any discussion of the self-consciousness of Jesus and his humanness must take into account his obedience to the will of the God whom he thought of as Father, an obedience by which he lived as well as one by which he died. Implicit in the synoptic depiction of Jesus, this total obedience is expressed more explicitly in John's Gospel, as we shall see later, in John's emphasis on the total dependence of the Son on the Father, and his subordination to him.

This brings us to the next aspect of Jesus' self-consciousness. Conscious of having been entrusted with a mission, and obediently setting himself to fulfil it in word, deed, life and death, Jesus is conscious too of a relationship, a special relationship, to the God who has entrusted him with the mission, the one whom he obeys implicitly. To quote Anderson again, "The question about Jesus is therefore the question about God."[22] This is the point to which all talk about the humanness of Jesus brings us in the end. It should not be necessary for me to go into detail about the place the idea of the Fatherhood of God has in the synoptic tradition or about the importance of the familiarity of the Aramaic "Abba" which Jesus used when he spoke to God. The insights of T. W. Manson[23] and Joachim Jeremias[24] on this question have been absorbed into contemporary discussion of synoptic theology, almost as a presupposition[25] without acknowledgement. The uniqueness of Jesus' manner of addressing God as "Abba" and speaking about him as "my Father" implies an awareness or belief on the part of Jesus that he stands in a special or unique relationship with God. We have to recognize with Jeremias that "there existed an increasing tendency to introduce the designation of God as Father into the sayings of Jesus,"[26] a fact which many years before had led T. W. Manson to speak of the fact that Jesus says very little about the Fatherhood of God, and "that only to a chosen few." "Rightly understood," he said, "this reticence is positive evidence of two things: the intense reality and deep sacredness of the experience itself, and the true manhood of Jesus."[27]

Awareness of this relationship with God, in which Jesus the man carries out his mission in a life of total obedience and dependence, finds its clearest synoptic expresssion in the accounts of the baptism (Mk, Mt, Lk), the temptations (Mt and Lk = Q), the transfiguration (Mk, Mt, Lk), the agony in Gethsemane (Mk, Mt and Lk), and most explicitly in the Q-saying,

Chapter III - Jesus in the Synoptic Gospels

> All things have been delivered to me by my Father; and
> no one knows the Son except the Father, and no one
> knows the Father except the Son and anyone to whom
> the Son chooses to reveal him (Mt 11:27 = Lk 10:22).

It is not possible to go into the vexed questions that surround
the background and authenticity of this saying, particularly
because of its apparent use of the absolute designation "the
Son" by Jesus himself. Nevertheless, it may confidently be
asserted that we do not have to rule out its authenticity on
the grounds that "the mutuality of relationship between the
Father and Son is a Hellenistic mystical idea that is quite
alien to Judaism," as W. G. Kümmel[28] and others have
done. W. D. Davies has shown that this kind of "I-Thou"
knowledge has its closest parallel in the "knowledge" of the
Dead Sea Scrolls.[29] Whether or not Jesus ever referred to
himself as "the Son" simpliciter, and even if this is a saying
elaborated by the church in transmission, there must lie
behind it a saying which implied a mutuality of relationship
between Jesus and God. Jeremias argues that Mt 11:27 should
be translated, "As only a father knows his son, so only a son
knows his father," and concludes that if this is correct, "then
Mt 11:27 is not a Johannine verse amidst synoptic material,
but rather one of those sayings from which Johannine
theology developed. Without such points of departure within
the synoptic tradition it would be an eternal puzzle how
Johannine theology could have originated at all."[30]

There is little evidence that in his awareness of his special
relationship with God Jesus saw any grounds for claiming a
special status for himself. The titles ascribed to him are
fundamentally functional, as many recent writers have
emphasized (e.g. H. Anderson,[31] J. A. T. Robinson,[32] E.
W. Saunders,[33] H. Küng,[34] W. Kasper[35]). Even if,
how- ever, it could be irrefutably demonstrated that Jesus
had claimed any of these "honorific titles" for himself, it
would not be possible to conclude that in so doing he was
making any ontological claim. Even the designations "Son of
Man," which I believe Jesus did use of himself, and "the
Messiah," about which there is good reason to be hesitant, do
not have any unmistakable ontological reference. As far as
the synoptic tradition is concerned Jesus, the man, is the
Messiah, the Son of God, the Son of David, the Prophet, and
so on, by virtue of his function in bringing good news of the

salvation, healing, renewal, recreation of man within the sovereign rule of God the Father. By his total self-giving to the mission which God has laid upon him, by his total obedience to God and total dependence on him, Jesus brings God near to men and men near to God. By his deeds and words he challenges men and women to enter into newness of life by becoming as little children, by committing themselves to a life of devoted discipleship, and so to share with him in the life of sonship.

This emphasis on the functional significance of Jesus' ministry as recorded in the Synoptics need not, however, rule out the possibility that in his exercise of these functions we may and can perceive something about Jesus himself. In much recent writing on christology, both by New Testament scholars, and by systematic theologians, a great deal is made of the presence of an "implicit christology" in the synoptic accounts. For example, R. H. Fuller, says that "the nearness of God is now a reality precisely in his drawing near in Jesus' eschatological ministry, which is therefore implicitly christological. Jesus can call God 'Abba' because he has known him as the one who has drawn nigh in his own word and deed, and he admits to the same privilege those who have responded to his own eschatological message."[36] Fuller goes on to say:

> An examination of Jesus's words - his proclamation of the Reign of God, and his call for decision, his enunciation of God's demand, and his teaching about the nearness of God - and of his conduct - his calling men to follow him and his healings, his eating with publicans and sinners - forces upon us the conclusion that underlying his word and work is an implicit christology. In Jesus as he understood himself, there is an immediate confrontation with "God's presence and his very self," offering judgment and salvation.[37]

The aspect of Jesus' activity in which the implicit christology comes most nearly to explicit expression is his authority (exousia). The authority with which Jesus speaks and acts is recognized by the crowds on a number of occasions; they acknowledge that his speech and action have an authority which their scribes lack (Mk 1:22 and parallels; Mk 1:27; Mt 9:8). The chief priests and elders recognize that Jesus acts with authority, but question its source, only to be placed on the horns of a dilemma by Jesus' question about the source of John's authority (Mk 11:28ff and parallels). Although the word "exousia" does nor occur in the Beelzebub controversy narrative (Mk 3:22ff and parallels), it is the same question of authority and the source of authority that is at issue. Indeed, the same holds good for the whole series of conflict stories which Mark conveniently brings together in chapters 2 and 3, in the first of which we have the explicit claim to authority by Jesus: "That you may know that the Son of Man has authority on earth to forgive sins," with the accompanying horror of the scribes who raised the cry of blasphemy, and the amazement of the crowd which glorified God (Mk 2:1-12). Jesus' authority is also recognized by the centurion whose servant was dying (Mt 8:9 = Lk 7:8). Further this authority which Jesus has makes itself plain in the way in which he prefixes solemn statements with the unprecedented and unparalleled formula, "Amen, I say to you," to which as Jeremias says, "the only substantial analogy ... is the messenger-formula 'Thus says the Lord', which is used by the prophets to show that their words are not their own wisdom, but a divine message."[38] This authority is to be seen in the way in which, at least according to Matthew, Jesus sets his word above that of "the fathers" and above that of Moses, in the antitheses of the Sermon on the Mount (Mt 5:21-48), and the claim to be greater than the temple, greater than Jonah, greater than Solomon (Mt 12:6 and parallels; Mt 12:41-42 and parallels). It is an authority which he is able to delegate to his disciples (Mk 3:15, 6:7 and parallels, Lk 10:19). And finally it is an authority which he demonstrates unmistakably when he drives the money-changers and dealers out of the temple.

Many recent writers stress that fact that Jesus for all his humanness - indeed in his very humanness - is "unique," "different," "provocative on all sides,"[39] at one with his fellow men, yet at the same time standing over against them and fitting no formula.[40] The provocative nature of his ministry, of the claims implicit in that mission, and of the authority with which he spoke and acted, challenges all his hearers. In Mark's narrative this provocativeness is a central theme, from Jesus' teaching in the synagogue on the sabbath in Mk 1:21, through the conflict stories of chapters 2 and 3, through Herod's puzzled questioning in chapter 6, the controversy with the Pharisees over ritual cleanliness in chapter 7 and sign-seeking in chapter 8, to the challenge to the disciples near Caesarea Philippi and the subsequent predictions of the passion. The provocation and the question of authority come to a head with the entry into Jerusalem, and the cleansing of the temple, which provoke the members of the Sanhedrin to ask about the source of his authority, and with Jesus' refusal to give an answer. The series of pericopae which follows, in which Pharisees and Herodians, Sadducees and scribes try to trap Jesus on a variety of issues - political (taxes), theological (resurrection) and religious (the greatest commandment) - leads to the silencing of the opposition and its discomfiture: "after that no one dared to ask him any question" (12:34), but "the great throng heard him gladly" (12:37). Thereafter, according to all the Gospels, events moved swiftly to the denouement of arrest, trial, crucifixion and burial. The Galilean teacher was threatening the delicate balance of Judean life under the Roman military governorship; he was challenging the authority of the Jewish leaders, he was subverting the nation, he was undermining the religion of the fathers, he was relativizing the Law which was the heart and soul of Judaism.

I have already said that I see no reason to doubt that Jesus foresaw that if he continued with his mission which he believed to be the will of his Father, it would lead inevitably to persecution and death. According to the whole Gospel tradition, echoed also in the letter to the Hebrews (5:7-10), Jesus shrank from the horror of the prospect of it, yet in obedience and trust submitted to it as his Father's will: "Not my will but yours be done" (Mk 14:36 and parallels). We must leave aside the question whether and in what sense Jesus' death was willed by God, but we cannot avoid the question what significance Jesus saw in the death that he knew would be the inevitable end of his mission. While there may be some grounds for doubting the authenticity of Mk 10:45, "to give his life a ransom for many," the Last Supper narratives leave no doubt that Jesus believed that his death would have covenantal significance, signifying, if not effecting, a new relationship between God and man, the beginning of a new community. Further, in Mark and Matthew, an explicit connection is made between this approaching death and the remission of sins. If Jesus made that connection, then he was not stating something new, for Deutero-Isaiah had spoken of the Servant of Yahweh being "wounded for our transgressions," "bruised for our iniquities," and making himself "an offering for sin" (Is 53:5,10); further it was a common Jewish belief that the death of the martyrs had vicarious atoning efficacy.

A serious mistake has been made, I believe, in much traditional doctrinal writing by relating atonement either solely to the death of Jesus, as if there were no forgiveness before his death, or solely to the incarnation (as some of the Fathers did) so that the death loses any special signficance. It is the whole Jesus-event which is significant, and the death, as part of that total event, takes its significance from the life it brought to an end. The death was not the death of any man; it was the death of this particular man, Jesus of Nazareth, who in voluntary obedience to God, had given himself entirely to the mission of proclaiming the nearness of God's Kingdom and of demanding from his hearers their obedient response to the call and claim he was making as the one sent by God.

Gerald O'Collins is right when he asserts that "no version of Calvary delivers a satisfactory form of theological goods unless it appreciates how Jesus went knowingly and willingly to his death,"[41] and he rightly criticizes Pannenberg for "playing down the voluntary obedience of Jesus."[42] Pannenberg indeed comes perilously close to monotheletism when he asserts that "the assumption that Jesus had the possibility of choice over against God's will is ... impossible ... as a consequence of Jesus' concrete historical existence in dedication to his mission"[43] at no point does he pay any attention to Jesus' agonizing in Gethsemane (Mk 14:36) except to note in passing that Jesus there chooses the Aramaic "Abba" to address God in prayer,[44] while he deals with the temptation of Jesus only in connection with Luther's interpretation of the penal suffering of Christ[45] and with fifth-century discussion of his sinlessness.[46] Nowhere does Pannenberg mention the temptation narratives of the synoptic Gospels, while Hebrews 4:15 about Jesus being "tempted in every respect as we are yet without sinning" only receives attention because of the last three words, "yet without sinning."[47] These two crucial events in the life of Jesus, however much their form may owe to the post-resurrection church, give the lie to any theology which denies Jesus' freedom of choice, the reality of his freedom as a man, and ultimately therefore the reality of his humanness.[48]

When we are dealing with the question of the significance which Jesus saw in his approaching death it is possible that a recent distinction may be of some assistance. Faced with the uncertainty about the authentic words of Jesus (ipsissima verba), J. Jeremias introduced the idea of the authentic voice of Jesus (ipsissima vox) which characterized Jesus' speech in ways "to which there is no analogy in contemporary literature,"[49] and which lead us to the very heart of "the ultimate mystery of the mission of Jesus."[50] Others have sought another route out of the impasse of the ipsissima verba by seeking to pin down "something of (Jesus') ipsissima intentio."[51] Thus Walter Kasper says that attempts "to show that Jesus himself attributed a soteriological effect to his death ... can only succeed if a convergence can be shown to exist between individual sayings and Jesus' general intention (ipsissima intentio)."[52] He proceeds to argue that this can be shown in two ways:

> (a) Jesus thought of his death in relation to his message of the coming of the Kingdom of God. The Kingdom of God involves salvation. Therefore Jesus saw his death as having saving significance.
> (b) In Jesus the Kingdom of God received "a personal embodiment in the form of service" - Jesus was among his disciples as one who serves (Lk 22:27). By this service Jesus brought healing to the alienated and guilt-ridden, liberation into a new community with God. "Service, ... living for others is the new way of living which Jesus inaugurated and made possible" and that involves risking your life even to the point of losing it (Mk 8:34-35 and pars). The Jewish idea of the representative and atoning death of the righteous man and the martyr pointed in the same direction. "In his life and in his death, Jesus is the man for others. Existing for others is his very essence. It is that which makes him the personified love of God for men."[53]

By this route of the ipsissima intentio, Kasper shows that it is legitimate to talk about Jesus' hidden or implicit soteriology as well as of his hidden or implicit christology. This motif of the intention of Jesus has been made the subject of an intensive study by Ben F. Meyer[54] who combines insights from Bernard Lonergan's philosophy of religion with the latest discussions of the synoptic witness to Jesus' understanding of his imminent death by J. Jeremias[55] and H. Schürmann.[56] Meyer argues that Jesus "himself grasped his imminent death ... as a constituent element of the messianic event."[57]

If it is granted, as I believe it must be, that Jesus expected his mission to end in violent death, and he saw that death as related to the Kingdom of God which he proclaimed and embodied, one final question remains to be discussed, and this relates not to the expectation of death but to the reality of Jesus' dying moments, in which the fullness of his humanity is to be clearly seen. It is strange how Christian tradition has from a very early stage refused to face the reality of Jesus' sense of being forsaken by God, expressed in the cry which Jesus uttered in the words of Psalm 22:1, "My God! My God! why have you forsaken me?" According to Mark and Matthew, "Jesus uttered a loud cry and expired" (Mk 15:37 = Mt 27:50), a cry which Küng says "corresponds to the fear and trembling before death mentioned by all three Synoptists (Mk 14:34 and pars), and toned down by Luke (22:43) with a reference to an angelic manifestation,[58] as a sign of God's closeness." Küng goes on to ask, "Is this the cry of someone praying confidently or of someone despairing of God?"[59] The "toning down" of Luke 22:43 (whether that verse belongs to the original text or not), is to be seen clearly in Luke's use of the triumphant strains of Ps 31:6, "Into thy hand I commend my spirit" as the final cry of Jesus, and further still in John 19:30, "It is consummated," with which "Jesus serenely gives up his spirit."[60] Jon Sobrino points out that in this way "the event of Jesus' death itself begins to lose its cutting edge in the very first efforts to interpret it. Somehow or other it was difficult right from the start to maintain the scandalous fact of abandonment by God that was embodied on Jesus' cross."[61] He proceeds to argue that what distinguishes the death of Jesus from other deaths, the death of a prophet or the martyrdom of a righteous man, is that "Jesus dies as the Son, as the one who proclaimed the nearness of his heavenly Father and then died completely abandoned by that Father."[62]

This scandal of the Father's abandonment of Jesus has not been taken seriously by later tradition because of the presupposition that such abandonment was literally impossible. Some Fathers, like Origen, Cyril of Alexandria, and Augustine, argued that the use of Psalm 22 by Jesus could only be metaphorical and he was speaking not for himself, but in the name of sinful humanity. Others, like Eusebius and Epiphanius, interpreted it "as a dialogue between Jesus' human nature and his divine nature." Yet another group, including Tertullian, Ambrose, and Thomas Aquinas "admitted that Jesus suffered abandonment by God, psychologically speaking; this caused him great anxiety, but not despair."[63] A detailed study of the history of the exegesis of "the cry of dereliction" (Mk 15:34) would most certainly be an interesting and illuminating exercise, as also would be an investigation of its interpretation in contemporary commentaries. There is little reason to doubt that the presupposition of the divinity of Jesus as Son of God has ruled out a priori for many the possibility that Jesus could feel abandoned by God. How could the second person of the Trinity feel abandoned by the first person? But such a question is anachronistic, resulting from the attempt to see the death of Jesus through Nicene and Chalcedonian eyes. Jesus dies <u>as the Son</u>, as Sobrino emphasizes. It is not only the man, Jesus, who dies; it is also the mission, the cause. Unlike prophets and martyrs, "Jesus dies in total <u>discontinuity</u> with his life and his cause. The death he experienced was not only the death of his person but also the death of his cause."[64] He died in complete and utter loneliness, abandoned by his own people, abandoned by his closest followers, abandoned by God, yet still clinging to the threads of a tattered faith, still able to cry, "My God!"

Out of all this varied witness of the synoptic tradition, when all due allowance has been made for the refraction of the tradition in the light of the post-resurrection faith, there emerges Jesus the man, impelled by his God-given mission, sustained by his relationship with God his Father whose will he obeys, acting with authority which comes from God, who is seen by the eyes of faith to be the one in whom God makes a new beginning for mankind. Jesus points those who will see and hear to a future of fullness of life with God which they can begin to know here and now, even as he knows it. He brings to them the wholeness, the salvation (soteria), the peace (shalom), which is God's will for his people.

Chapter IV

HUMANNESS IN THE EARLY PREACHING AND PAUL

E NOTED, in the first lecture, the controversy which followed the Uppsala Assembly of the World Council of Churches over the implications of the emphasis on "humanization" for the theology of mission. We saw how Peter Beyerhaus interpreted it as "the replacement of Theology by Anthropology,"[1] and we saw how M. M. Thomas replied by emphasizing that "Christian missionary thinking cannot be either theology or anthropology except as either of them is related to Christology ... If it is Christ-centred, anthropology could become truly Christian in its framework."[2] Up to this point I have refrained from making observations about what constitutes humanness or trying to define "man" except insofar as, from my excursion into the Old Testament and Jewish thought in the second lecture, I came to the conclusion that the basic contribution of Jewish anthropology is the relationality of man. The emphasis is on man, not as an individual, but on man in relationship with the God who creates, loves, redeems and gives him a basis for hope; in relationship with the rest of the created order as the one to whom it is given to have dominion over it; in relationship with other human beings - the man-woman relationship, relationship within the family, tribe, nation and so on. Similarly in our attempt to see the Jesus of the synoptic Gospels we noted the centrality of the idea of relationality, not as an abstract "theologoumenon," but as the portrayal of the concrete relationships in which Jesus makes known the reality of his humanness and offers to men and women the gracious possibility of themselves coming to fullness of humanness in relationship with him, and through him with God.

57

I have refrained, however, from any kind of analytical anthropology, by which I mean the listing of characteristics which differentiate man from God on the one side, and from what is neither God nor man on the other. There is a danger in approaching the question who Jesus was or is by this kind of check-list method. Walter Kasper,[3] echoing Hans Urs von Balthasar,[4] calls this the error of setting Jesus Christ in "a predetermined scheme of reference." It is to set out some definition of what it is to be a man and then to discuss how far Jesus measures up to the definition, whereas, if Jesus Christ is the centre of the Christian faith, our starting point in thinking about his humanity must be with Jesus himself as he is witnessed to in the New Testament and in the continuing tradition of the Church.

It is for that reason, too, that I have refrained from dealing with the so-called christological or honorific titles, for these also can dangerously become "a predetermined frame of reference." Research into the background of the various titles by the "religionsgeschichtlich" method is a fascinating pastime, and has provided topics for countless doctoral dissertations and will continue to do so. In the last analysis, however, the titles do not tell us who Jesus is. It is not the titles that give meaning to Jesus Christ, but Jesus Christ who fills the titles with meaning.[5] Therefore, in my last lecture on the synoptic witness to Jesus, I tried to get at some hints about how Jesus saw himself through what is implicit in his fulfilment of his mission, in his obedience and awareness of intimate relationship with God, in the authority with which he taught and acted, and in his faithfulness to his cause even to the utter loneliness and abandonment of the cross. We saw him as one who lived entirely for God and for his cause, which is the well-being of man, and in doing so lived also entirely for his fellow-men with whom he identified himself, and to whom he offered God's gracious gift of forgiveness, healing, wholeness and reconciliation. We saw him as the one who, at the end, was crucified by his enemies, forsaken by family and friends, and felt himself to be abandoned by God.

This leads us now to the crunch question which every christology must face, to what Küng calls "the most problematic point of our study of Jesus of Nazareth,"[6] the question of the relationship between the Jesus of history and the Christ of faith, the question of "Jesus and Christian

Origins," how it came about that "it was only after Jesus' death that the movement invoking his name really started."[7] It is not my intention, even if we had the time, to make an exhaustive study of the varying interpretations of the resurrection of Jesus from the dead. Even in the New Testament itself there is a variety of interpretations of the nature of the resurrection, corresponding to the variety of expectations of resurrection that existed in contemporary Judaism. In and through all the variety, however, there is a unity of witness to the fact that the Jesus who died forsaken and abandoned "is encountered as a living person by the disciples."[8] They accounted for this fact in thought-forms drawn from their own religious background in terms of resurrection or exaltation or a combination of both. However we may try to explain it, there was no doubt in the minds of the disciples that the living person who enountered them was none other than the Jesus who had been crucified by the Roman administration at the instigation of the Jewish authorities on a charge of political subversion. The method of execution and the inscription on the cross establish the charge: "He was executed as a claimant to Kingship (= a messianic pretender)."[9] Yet the crucifixion of Jesus as "the King of the Jews" tells us no more than that this is the way the authorities interpreted his missionary activity, but nothing at all about Jesus' self-understanding or about the disciples' understanding of him.

How then do we get from the tragically ended life and mission of Jesus to the proclamation of the disciples that Jesus has been raised from the dead? Leaving aside any of our presuppositions of faith, we still have to ask, "What must be supposed in order to account for the very emergence of the Church's christological confession? ... What must be supposed of the (pre-paschal and paschal) consciousness of the proclaimers, if we are to account for the coming into being of their specifically messianic proclamation?"[10] The disciples did not suddenly and very shortly after Good Friday simply declare that Jesus' cause was right in spite of his execution as a criminal; rather we find that Jesus' death and the abhorrent instrument which was the means of that death have suddenly and very soon become the main theme of faith "through its connection with the claim that Jesus was raised from the dead by God."[11] Many scholars have written much about "the Easter experience of the disciples"; the appearances of the risen Jesus would not, without some prior preparation, have suggested to them the idea that Jesus was the Messiah.[12] There is no evidence of any connection in Jewish thought beteen the ideas of Messiahship and resurrection, just as there is no evidence of any connection between the ideas of Messiahship and martyrdom, although there is evidence for the idea of instant resurrection of the martyrs.[13] Meyer accuses the form critics of turning "the Easter experience of the disciples into "a magic top-hat from which, like so many rabbits, there unexpectedly emerged the church itself, its messianic proclamation and its basic soteriology."[14] The most logical source for the connection between messiahship, martyrdom and resurrection is to be found in the Gospel tradition, in the implicit christology and soteriology of Jesus himself, which began to become explicit when the disciples were confronted by the risen Jesus. That is to say, the source is to be found in the implicit christology or messianology of the ministry of Jesus, and in the fact that he predicted martyrdom and resurrection as the outcome of his mission, even though the details of the predictions have certainly been made more explicit in the light of what had actually happened.[15]

Whatever it was that happened and whatever the imagery used to describe it, something "happened" with such explosive and creative force that its shock waves are still being felt in the lives of men and women two thousand years later; the so-called "apotheosis" of the crucified Jesus, to quote Martin Hengel, "must already have taken place in the forties, and one is tempted to say that more happened in this period of less than two decades than in the whole of the next seven centuries, up to the time when the doctrine of the early church was completed."[16] This "happening" or "event" - and I realize that the use of these terms will be questioned - the first followers of Jesus, as Jews by birth and nurture, described in such apocalyptic terms as "resurrection" or "exaltation." It was the "resurrection" of the Jesus whose disciples they had been and this was the focal point of the missionary preaching on which they embarked. Central to the missionary proclamation in the Acts of the Apostles, whatever the sources of the "speeches" may be, was the declaration that "Jesus of Nazareth, a man ..., this Jesus, you crucified and killed ... But God raised him up" (Acts 2:22-24); "this Jesus God raised up, and of that we are all witnesses"

(Acts 2:32); "God has made him both Lord and Christ, this Jesus whom you crucified" (Acts 2:36); "the God of our fathers glorified his servant (or child - "pais") Jesus ... God raised him from the dead" (Acts 3:13,15) - and so we could go on through the speeches. Graham Stanton,[17] along with others, has emphasized the pre-Lucan traditions behind the speeches, and draws the conclusion that "Peter's speeches in Acts make it quite clear that the early church did not proclaim Jesus of Nazareth without at the same time proclaiming him as the Risen One, Lord and Christ; nor did it proclaim the Risen Christ and side-step or minimise the significance of the pre-resurrection events and the character of the One who was raised from the dead."[18] Even when we turn to Paul's Areopagus speech (Acts 17:22-31), the authenticity or historicity of which has been questioned most seriously, the final emphasis falls on "a man whom he has appointed ... of this he has given assurance to all men by raising him from the dead" (17:31).

The same emphasis is to be found in the fragments of hymns and confessions and acclamations embedded in the writings of Paul and his school. The Risen Lord whom Paul proclaims is the Jesus of Nazareth "who was descended from David according to the flesh" (Rom 1:4); the Christ who "died for our sins in accordance with the scriptures, ... was buried ... was raised on the third day" (I Cor 15:3f). "He humbled himself and became obedient unto death, even death on a cross. Therefore God has highly exalted him ... that at the name of Jesus every knee should bow" (Phil 2:8,9), while in the so-called "cosmic" christology of Col 1:15ff the one who is declared to be "the image of the invisible God, the first-born of all creation" (v.15) is also said to be "the first-born from the dead" (v.18) through whom God makes "peace by the blood of his cross" (v.20). The identity of the Risen Lord is always the man who was crucified, and it is to that man that all the titles of honour are ascribed.

The desire to preserve the continuity of the Risen Lord with the man, Jesus of Nazareth, may be one of the motives that led the early church to develop the stories of the empty tomb, which emphasize the continuity and identity by depicting the resurrection body of Jesus as being the body that had been laid in the tomb, either the same body, or a renewed body, or a transformed or spiritualized body. On the nature of the resurrection body there is considerable diversity of opinion in the New Testament, and even Paul reflects a diversity of views which cannot be completely harmonized or reconciled with each other; that is only to be expected in view of the diversity of opinion that existed in Jewish expectation of the resurrection.[19] The same desire to maintain continuity probably accounts for the process of "materialization" of the appearances of the Risen Lord, with John having Jesus, who had just passed through closed doors, inviting doubting Thomas to put his finger in the nail prints (John 20:27), and with Luke having the Risen Lord eating a piece of fish. The latter was something which James Denney found "not only incongrous but repellent."[20]

This emphasis on continuity is carried still further with the idea of the bodily ascension of the Risen Lord, which only Luke records (Lk 24:50ff; Acts 1:9-11) and with the doctrine of the permanent manhood of Christ which D. M. Baillie describes as a "traditional catholic doctrine," and which he uses as an argument against the kenotic theory of the incarnation. Quoting the "Westminster Shorter Catechism" (Answer to Q.21) which speaks of Christ "who, being the eternal Son of God, became man, and so was, and continueth to be, God and man in two distinct natures, and one person, for ever," Baillie argued that to maintain that Christ's human nature ended "when the days of his flesh on earth ended ... would make nonsense of the Incarnation."[21] Later, when discussing "The Legacy of the Incarnation," Baillie asserts that this idea is an essential element of belief in the incarnation and the Chalcedonian doctrine of the two distinct natures united in the one person of Christ.[22] He admits the difficulty of interpreting this doctine; I can see some attractiveness about the notion but have failed to discover any attempt anywhere to trace its biblical or patristic origins or to give any satisfactory justification for it as essential to belief in incarnation.

Similarly there is an attractiveness about Karl Barth's view that the human nature of Christ existed before the incarnation,[23] in that it, too, like the notion of permanent post-existence, takes the reality and importance of the humanness of Jesus with the utmost seriousness. But just as the notion of permanent post-existence of the human nature raises the difficult question what exactly this human nature is which continues to exist, so also does the notion ot its pre-existence. I suspect that when this kind of question is being asked we are still enmeshed in the thought-forms of Greek metaphysics; I see a close parallel between these notions of the human nature and the Platonic doctrine of the pre-existence and post-existence of the soul which Origen made into a keystone of his whole doctrinal system. The question of pre-existence will arise again, but here we simply note these ideas which have been used to stress the centrality of the humanness of Jesus.

We must return to those two decades in which, as Martin Hengel says, so much happened in the development of the doctrine of the person of Jesus Christ. The key figure in this period must of course be the apostle Paul who carried the gospel of God's reconciling action in Christ to the gentile world. The mystery of the transformation of the terrified, disillusioned disciples into fearless proclaimers that God has raised Jesus from the dead - the mystery to which we give the name "resurrection" - is matched by the mystery of the conversion of a Pharisee of the Pharisees and persecutor of the church to become the apostle to the gentiles.[24] While Paul's conversion in many ways parallels the call of prophets of the Old Testament, in no Old Testament prophetic call is there such a complete "volte face" as that which happened to Paul, involving a complete transformation of theological stance and religious attitude, a complete transvaluation of values, or what Charles Kannengiesser calls "the trans-mutation of the traditional values of Judaism into the terms of the Gospel."[25] Paul underwent an experience that was so profound and so radical that he could only describe it as "a new creation" (kainê ktisis) (II Cor 5:17; Gal 6:15). "He who once persecuted" the church "is now preaching the faith he once tried to destroy" (Gal 1:23).

A vast amount has been written about Paul's view of salvation and the anthropology that is implied in it. It would be more correct however to say that Paul's anthropology is derived from his understanding of Jesus (the Jesus-event of life, death and resurrection) and of the nature of Jesus' humanness, and that his view of salvation, or his different images of salvation, are his attempt to explain the relationship between Jesus' humanness and that of the Christian. Of course Paul expressed his understanding of the Christ-event and of salvation in concepts derived from his background in Judaism (Palestinian or Hellenistic), but the association of those concepts with the Christ-event fills the concepts with new content. It may be true that Paul has little to say explicitly in his letters about the details of Jesus' life and teaching, but it is erroneous to argue on the basis of his letters either that he knew little or nothing, or that he deliberately dismissed what he did know as irrelevant to the gospel he had to preach.[26] The correct exegesis of II Cor 5:16 is still being debated; many interpret the "according to the flesh" (kata sarka) as referring to the earthly Jesus and not to Paul's way of looking at Jesus "from a human point of view." Little attention is paid to the context and the first part of the verse in which Paul says that from now on, since the death and resurrection of Jesus, "we no longer regard anyone 'kata sarka'." Since we have become Christians, and in the light of the death and resurrection of Jesus, our attitude towards both Jesus and our fellow men is different from what it was before. As Murphy-O'Connor says:

> He had possessed an inferior type of knowledge of Jesus. All this can mean in the light of what he says about his persecution of the Church (Phil 3:6) is that he at one time shared the estimation of Jesus common among his contemporaries, namely that he was an heretical teacher and a turbulent agitator whose activities had with justice brought him to the scaffold. This, Paul now recognizes, was a false judgment, which he has now abandoned ... He has also abandoned a similar way of judging others ... [Now] Christ's pattern of behaviour is the standard by which Christians must judge the quality of life of others. Consequently, if anyone is "in Christ" he must judge in a new way ... A new standard or point of reference has been accepted, namely "the love of Christ" by which Paul himself is now constrained (II Cor 5:14). Paul does not exaggerate when he speaks of this as a "new creation."[27]

Further, it is too frequently overlooked that the letters of Paul cannot be taken as examples, either in form or content, of Pauls's missionary preaching. In writing, usually to churches which he had founded by his preaching, Paul assumes that his readers have some memories of what he had preached, and on occasions he reminds them of particular points of his preaching, but he sees no need to repeat its full content, and certainly no reason to turn his letters into evangelistic sermons.[28]

Nonetheless it cannot be denied that for Paul it is the cross and the resurrection that form the pivot of the gospel and the basis of his exhortation to his churches. It may be considered somewhat out of date and too reminiscent of the old liberal gospel against which Karl Barth reacted so violently sixty years ago to emphasize that the notion of Jesus as a "model" or "example" plays an important role in Paul's theology and exhortation, and yet the theme is important and appears most often in contexts where Paul is striving to drive home some point of exhortation - to humility, to unity, to obedience - with strong theological support. He presents Christ as the model, imitation of whom leads to, produces, inspires, creates authentic individual and corporate humanness. The exhortation to imitate, however, implies a difference between our humanness and that real, genuine, authentic humanness of Christ which Paul says we are to imitate.

In order to understand this more fully and to avoid falling into the trap of the old liberal humanistic gospel of the beginning of the century, we have to look more closely at what Paul has to say about the relation between Christ's humanness and ours. To do this it is necessary to look at a number of passages in Paul's letters, all of which are exegetically hot issues. It will not be possible to deal with them in detail; all we can do is to state the position which seems most viable. In what follows I find myself strongly influenced by the recent work of Jerome Murphy-O'Connor,[29] who has argued that the key to understanding Paul's thinking about authentic humanity or genuine humanness is to be found in the linkages in Jewish thought between three concepts: the concept of "the righteous man" in the Wisdom literature (particularly in "The Wisdom of Solomon"), the Suffering Servant of Deutero-Isaiah (and the Psalms of the Righteous Sufferer), and Adam in the Yahwistic creation-narrative in Genesis chs. 2-3) (with overtones of the Priestly narrative of Genesis ch.1).

In the Yahwistic narrative Adam, prior to the Fall, was man as God intended him to be. "Jewish tradition, represented by Philo and the intertestamental literature, believed that Adam prior to the Fall was the perfect embodiment of the divine intent for humanity."[30] While in the canonical Old Testament, as we have seen, the Yahwistic narrative seems to have played no part, extra-canonical thought in late pre-Christian Judaism, prompted by awareness of the imperfection of sinful humanity, and by the eschatological hope that the End would be as the Beginning, began to construct a portrait of Adam in his perfect humanness in a paradisaical setting in terms of which is described the future that was yet to be.

Paul was influenced by this Adamic speculation, as W. D. Davies[31], C. K. Barrett[32], and Robin Scroggs[33] and others have demonstrated, but he was forced to modify it because of his awareness of the new beginning that God had made in his life through his encounter with the Risen Christ. Because of the universality of sin in humanity and of sin's power over fallen humanity, as Murphy-O'Connor argues, "a new creation was necessary to restore to humanity an authentic exemplar of the divine intention. There had to be a perfect individual who would be all that God desired humanity to be, and Paul found him in Christ. He, as the Last Adam, was the visibility of God's intention. He was what Adam was created to be."[34] In the light of this insight it is possible to come to a clearer understanding of the much debated anthropological passage in Romans 7:7 - 8:4. The "I" of this passage is not an individual - Paul - but humanity, and humanity's religious history is divided into three periods. Murphy-O'Connor shows that if this passage is read in the light of the Yahwist's creation narrative the three periods are quite clearly:

1. Humanity before the Fall (7:7-13)
2. Humanity between the Fall and Christ (7:14-24)
3. Humanity after the advent of Christ (7:25 - 8:4)

The first and third periods are characterized by "life" (authentic existence) and the middle period by "death" (inauthentic existence).[35] In another passage there are specific contacts with the Priestly narrative: II Cor 4:4-6, which speaks of "the light of the gospel of the glory of Christ, who is the image of God ... it is the God who said, "Let light shine out of darkness," who has shone in our hearts to give the light of the knowledge of the glory of God in the face of Christ." Here Christ is declared to be "the image of God," God is the creator of light, and Christ is said to possess the glory of God. (The latter idea is a development of the Creation narrative in late Jewish literature). "Christ has, therefore, what Adam lost. He is the New Adam who perfectly embodies the authentic humanity that was the goal of God's creative act!"[36]

This line of interpretation also throws light on another much discussed passage, the "cosmological hymn" of Colossians 1:15-20, which brings together the ideas of "creation" and "image of God"; it is to be noted, however, that Paul (or a disciple?) keeps this high-flying christology firmly anchored to earth by setting it in soteriological brackets: v.13: "He has delivered us from the dominion of darkness and transferred us to the kingdom of his beloved Son, in whom we have redemption, the forgiveness of sins, who is the image of the invisible God, the first-born of all creation ... vv 21-22. And you ... he has now reconciled in his body of death." Within the cosmic terminology, the emphasis is on humanity, on Jesus who is "the first-born of all creation," as the man Jesus, "the image of the invisible God." It is a mistake to read into this hymn the idea of personal pre-existence as it came to be formulated in later christological dogma. Any idea of pre-existence here must be interpreted in the light of Jewish ideas of pre-existence in the mind of God, a notion found in Rabbinic and Wisdom Literature which, in scholastic theology, was described as "examplar causality,"[37] which can easily be confused with the platonic doctrine of forms (but probably owes nothing to it). As Murphy-O'Connor puts it, "In order to create Adam, God must have had an idea of perfect humanity. For Christians, that perfect humanity was conceived only in Christ. Christ, therefore, was conceived to represent the divine intent which came to historical expression in the creation of Adam."[38] It is as "the first-born of all creation" that he is also "the beginning, the first-born from the dead," and "the head of the body, the church" (Col 1:18).[39]

In another important passage with a strongly cosmological flavour, Romans 8, the ideas of creation and new creation are linked with soteriology and eschatology, with election, justification and sanctification. In the midst of it all Paul speaks of God predestining some "to be conformed to the image of his Son, in order that he might be the first-born of many brethren" (Rom 8:29). Thus we have the interrelation of ideas of Christ as the first-born of all creation, the first-born from the dead, the first-born of many brethren. That is, in Christ God has made a fresh start with humanity, and henceforth fullness of humanity is to be seen in Christ, and "if any one is in Christ, he is a new creation; the old has passed away, behold, the new has come, and all this is from God who through Christ reconciled us to himself" (II Cor 5:17-18).

We must look at one final passage which is still the arena of much debate. This one occurs, not in a soteriological setting, but in a strictly paraenetic, or exhortatory setting. Almost without doubt originally an early hymn with a definitely un-Pauline sound and language, the Kenosis-passage of Philippians 2:6-11 is used in an attempt to encourage or persuade the Philippians to move always toward greater unity of mind and love among themselves by imitating the humility, the self-humiliation of Jesus. This is not the place to enter into discussion of the original form of the hymn, for our concern is with what the words mean in their context in Philippians. If Murphy-O'Connor's argument is right - and I think in its main outline it certainly is - then we are intended to see Christ "as the Righteous Man par excellence" of the Wisdom tradition, and as such "the perfect image of God ... totally what God intended man to be" (en morphêi theou); "his sinless condition gave him the right to be treated as if he were a god" (to einai isa theôi), "that is to enjoy the incorruptibility in which Adam was created" (Wisd. Sol. 2:23). But Jesus did not try to use this right for his own advantage but gave himself up "to a mode of existence that was not his by accepting the condition of a slave which involved suffering and death." As a man Jesus was like other men, indeed identical with them, and yet he differed from them because, being sinless, he did not need to be reconciled to God. "Nonetheless, he humbled himself in obedience and accepted death. Therefore God has highly exalted (super-exalted) him and given him the title and authority that had hitherto been God's alone."[40] Murphy O'Connor's aim is to find the meaning of the original hymn; he says it is "an attempt to define the uniqueness of Christ considered precisely as man ... He was thus led to see the uniqueness of Jesus in terms of his sinlessness."[41]

As a hymn with such an emphasis Paul could well approvingly quote it as an example of humility which must be the basis of unity among Christians. Whether the words "even death on a cross" (v.8) are considered as a Pauline interpolation (as with Jeremias,[42] Murphy-O'Connor[43] and

68

many others), or treated an as integral part of the hymn as by Martin Hengel,[44] for whom "even death on a cross" emphasizes the full force of what it meant to take the form of a slave, namely, to accept a form of death reserved for slaves, the emphasis in the hymn is on the active, voluntary obedience even to death on the part of the one who did not need to die. As Paul says elsewhere, "While we were still weak, at the right time Christ died for the ungodly ... God shows his love for us in that while were were yet sinners Christ died for us" (Rom 5:6,8), and elsewhere again, "For our sake he made him to be sin who knew no sin" (II Cor 5:21). So ultimately the death of Christ is the means by which God in his love saves us, renewing us in the image of his Son, redeeming us from slavery through him who took the form of a slave, reconciling us to himself, removing the barrier of alienation and enmity.

In the context of Philippians, if we accept the letter as a single letter as it now stands, Paul reinforces the argument for humility which he had illustrated by the self-humiliation of Christ, by setting out in chapter 3 how he himself had had to "empty himself" of everything of value that was his either by inheritance or by achievement in order that he might "gain Christ and be found in him, not having a righteousness of [his] own, but that which is through faith in Christ, the righteousness from God that depends on faith" (Phil 3:8-9). Paul emphasizes that he had not yet arrived, but is pressing on towards the goal (vv.12f), and then urges the Philippians to join in imitating him. Thus Paul sees a parallelism between the fullness of Jesus' humanity which is a fact demonstrated in his life and death and resurrection, and the fullness of humanity which will be his (Paul's) when he attains the resurrection of the dead.[45]

This parallelism which Paul sees between what Jesus was and is and what the believer is destined to be and will be, along with his emphasis on the believer's imitation of Christ or being "conformed to his image" (Rom 8:29) leads us on to a further point which must be made. We have already noted the tension or oscillation in Hebrew thought between emphasis on the individual and emphasis on the community, and the concept usually referred to as "corporate personality." We westerners, nurtured in the classical-renaissance-enlightenment tradition of individualism find this concept a difficult one to comprehend, yet it is a pivotal concept in many non-western traditions - for example in the religious traditions of Africa, of the East and of the peoples of the Pacific.

The growing importance of the individual in late pre-Christian Jewish thought was not allowed to obscure the awareness of the community and the belief that it is only in and with the community that the individual can find his real humanity in relationship with God. This idea remains central in the synoptics with Jesus gathering twelve disciples as the nucleus of the new people of God, with his proclamation of the Kingdom of God which involves a community over which God rules as sovereign, with his emphasis on the establishment of a new covenant.

This relationship is also central in Paul's thought. To be sure his initial experience of Christ was vividly and radically individual - that is emphasized in all accounts of his conversion or call. But at the same time Paul was aware that this experience was one of being incorporated into a new community, and this experience he interpreted in terms of reconciliation; he knew that he was no longer at enmity with God, but that God had reconciled him to himself and at the same time brought him into the right relationship with his fellow men. Paul uses a variety of images or metaphors to describe the "how" of this process - justification, redemption, salvation, adoption, sacrificial offering and so on. None of them by itself is adequate, nor are all of them together, yet each and all emphasize that, in Jesus Christ, God has acted to bring us into a new relationality, into that relationality which we see in Jesus' life, teaching, death and resurrection, which Jesus not only exemplifies but somehow creates in those who respond to God through him.

The importance of this idea of finding humanity in community is to be seen in at least two facets of Paul's theology. The first is his concept of being "in Christ," that phrase which he uses so often and which has been the cause of so much debate. Like C. F. D. Moule,[46] I find this phrase a puzzle, and like him I think it has to be linked with the idea of corporate personality, although I am not sure that I can go along with his idea that this means that Jesus Christ is more than individual, and that is is in that that Jesus' uniqueness lies. Certainly the concept "in Christ" is closely connected with the image of the Church as "the body of Christ," and Paul's use of that image stresses the importance

70

of community, interdependence, relationality in the life of the Christian as the place in which the believer finds his real humanity.

Let it not be thought that this emphasis on the humanness of Jesus as being the paradigm of the humanness, the authentic humanity, which is God's intention for human beings, diminishes in any way the divine aspect of the person and work of Jesus Christ in Paul's theology, or indeed anywhere else in the New Testament. For Paul, Jesus is Christ, Lord, Son of God; for him "God was in Christ" (II Cor 5:19), and "Jesus Christ the Lord" stands alongside "God our Father" in the opening greetings of letter after letter (Rom 1:7; I Cor 1:2; Gal 1:3; [Eph 1:2]; Phil 1:2; I Thess 1:1; [II Thess 1:2]; I Tim 1:2; II Tim 1:2; [Titus 1:4]; Philem 3). Paul has not said all that God means to him until he has said "Father and Son"; indeed not until he has said, "Father, Son and Holy Spirit" (II Cor 13:14). What Jesus was, was the doing of God; what Jesus is and does is the doing of God: "God shows his love for us in that while we were yet sinners Christ died for us" (Rom 5:8) The divine-human dichotomy of later christology would have been almost incomprehensible to Paul. Jesus Christ, for him, is God's self-humanization for the humanization of mankind. So there comes a point where "christology-from-below" becomes also "christology-from-above," an identification to which we are driven as we give worship and praise to God the Father through Jesus Christ his Son our Lord.

Chapter V

HUMANNESS IN HEBREWS AND JOHN

REPEATEDLY in a series of lectures given in New Zealand and Australia in 1966 under the title "Jesus in the Variegated Witness of the New Testament," which was an embryonic version of his book "Jesus,"[1] Eduard Schweizer emphasized the variety of New Testament witness to Jesus. He spoke about the confusing wealth of christological concepts, and emphasized, as he does in the book, that Jesus is "the Man who fits no formula"[2] - no single New Testament formula and no single ecclesiastical formula - and that "the church must continue to make fresh statements of who Jesus is."[3] The diversity of the New Testament, not only on the subject of christology but on practically every aspect of theology and praxis, has become axiomatic in biblical studies to such an extent that one of the liveliest debates today concerns the question wherein lies the unity.[4] This diversity has rightly become a presupposition of most contemporary writing on christology. To give but one example, Jon Sobrino says "the New Testament presents not one but several different christologies." The same writer a little later points out that "the diverse christologies of the New Testament were elaborated from two poles. Jesus of Nazareth was one pole. The other was the concrete situation of each community."[5] What he says about the diverse New Testament christologies applies to christologies in every community and in every age.

Certainly the study of New Testament christologies bears out Sobrino's view of their bipolarity, and despite the shortcomings or excesses of form and redaction criticism, the importance of the triple "Sitze-im-Leben" of the gospel material has been adequately demonstrated: the setting in the life of Jesus, the setting in the life of the community which preserved and used the Jesus-tradition, and the setting in which the particular evangelist puts it and the use he makes of it within his redactional framework. But it is not only the Gospels that give us these glimpses of the ways in which the Jesus-tradition is transmitted and developed and applied. We have seen how the early preaching in Acts harks back to the deeds and words, the death and resurrection of Jesus, and similarly how Paul takes hold of the tradition and applies it paraenetically to his own situation or to that of the church to which he is writing. Further, if Colossians and Ephesians are deutero-Pauline rather than Pauline, they give us further glimpses of this bipolarity of christology. The Jesus-tradition is kept alive, not simply by being recorded in gospel narrative form, but also by being appealed to, repeated, applied to the very diverse situations to which the early missionaries addressed themselves in the primitive Christian communities. Indeed the tradition is a living tradition and continues to live as, and in so far as, it is handed on in the living situation of the living, worshipping, witnessing community.

While we are discussing this point it is necessary for us to take a further step. It is clear from the Gospels that there was not from the beginning a single Jesus-tradition, but that there existed a number of divergent though overlapping traditions, and that some of these were used by the evangelists as they composed their Gospels (see Luke 1:1-4). Put in its simplest terms, different individuals remembered different things about what Jesus did and said, or maybe remembered some of the same things in slightly different ways, and passed on their memories of Jesus in the communities with which they were associated. In different communities, with their "different concrete situations," different uses would be made of their traditions and different emphases given. Eventually some traditions tended to become normative and were harmonized into a single tradition, but that did not necessarily mean that the other traditions were completely displaced or forgotten. Thus, by the end of the second century we find Irenaeus and Tertullian appealing to "the rule of faith," the "regula fidei," while in the fourth century Athanasius appeals to both the "regula fidei" (kanôn tês pisteôs) and "the scope of scripture" (skopos tôn graphôn). To return to New Testament times, despite the insights of C. H. Dodd into "the apostolic preaching and its de-

74

velopments,"[6] there is now general agreement that it is in fact impossible to elicit a single apostolic kerygma from the New Testament writings. From the beginning there has been variety and diversity both in the tradition about Jesus and in the faith-response to that tradition in the church's proclamation of the gospel.

This variety and diversity is clearly to be seen in the synoptic Gospels and within the Pauline corpus itself. We get further glimpses of it in the rest of the New Testament writings, where we find the various writers making their own idiosyncratic use of their memories of Jesus or those of their own particular communities.[7] In the rest of this lecture I want to look in some detail at two of these writers and their communities; the Johannine literature coming from "The Community of the Beloved Disciple," to quote the title of Raymond Brown's recent fascinating book[8] - the literature which has played the dominant role in the development of christology - and "The Letter to the Hebrews," whose contribution to ecclesiastical christology has been minimal, except for the use made of it in elucidating the priestly work of Christ. Again attention will be focused on the humanness of Jesus, even though both these writers appear to set their thinking about Jesus in the framework of "christologies-from-above."

It is appropriate to juxtapose Hebrews and the Fourth Gospel for they display some quite remarkable similarities as well as striking dissimilarities. Of the Letter to the Hebrews, Markus Barth commented, "No other book of the New Testament (except the Fourth Gospel) puts the real deity and true humanity of Jesus Christ so clearly side by side."[9] Others have frequently pointed out the intense interest Hebrews has in the humanness of Jesus and the central role it plays in his argument.[10] Cullmann can even talk of the author of Hebrews having "the courage to speak of Jesus in shockingly human terms," while stressing, like Markus Barth, that "at the same time he emphasized perhaps more strongly than any other the deity of the Son."[11]

The "Sitz-im-Leben," both of the author of "Hebrews" and of the community (or communities) for which he writes his treatise, can only be deduced from the writing itself. We do not know who the author is. We do not know for whom he was writing. We do not know when he wrote. The answers to these questions must be deduced from the treatise, and can be considered no more than hypothetical; as a result a wide variety of answers has been given and no agreement reached. Certainly the community is undergoing a crisis of confidence; its faith is being tested, and some of its members have committed apostasy or are in danger of doing so (Heb 6:6-8).[12] It appears that they are in danger of lapsing back into Judaism - whether they were Palestinian Jewish Christians or Hellenistic Jewish Christians is probably no more than an academic question, for it is no longer possible to draw a clear line between the two as I. H. Marshall[13] and Martin Hengel[14] have shown over against the too facile distinction which the history-of-religions school had made a dominant pre-supposition for so long.[15] Having been won over to Christian faith from Judaism, under pressure of some kind, whether persecution or sympathy for the Jewish community to which they had formerly belonged, they are in danger of turning back from their new faith to their old.

To restore their confidence, to renew their faith, and to prevent them from falling away, the author sets out to remind them of the superiority of the new covenant, which God has established "in these last days" (1-2) over the old covenant. This new covenant (8:13; 9:15; 12:24) is also a better covenant (7:22; 8:6) and an eternal covenant (13:20). Its superiority over the old is demonstrated in a variety of ways, cultic, ethical and religious, while as the "eternal" covenant it is seen as the fulfilment and perfection (teleiôsis) of the eternal covenant which Yahweh made with the patriarchs (Gen 9:16; 17:13,19 etc.). The superiority of the new is clearly stated in the opening verses: "In many and various ways God spoke of old to our fathers by the prophets; but in these last days he has spoken to us by a Son"(1:1-2). It is God's speaking through a Son that has made all the difference, a Son who is superior to angels, to Moses, to the Levitical priesthood, a Son whose sacrificial blood is superior to that of the sacrifices of the old covenant, and so on. Yet, having started with this statement which is clearly a christology-from-above, it is significant that so much of the treatise is focused on the man Jesus;[16] in seeking to renew the faith and re-establish the confidence of his readers, the author directs their attention to the human name, Jesus. Westcott points out that this name, unattached to any title, occurs nine times, and "in every case it furnishes the key to the argument of the passage where it is found."[17] "We see Jesus ... crowned with glory and honour" (2:9); "consider Jesus, the apostle and high priest of our faith" (3:1); "Jesus the forerunner" (6:20); "Jesus the surety of a better covenant" (7:22); "Jesus, the pioneer and perfecter of faith" (12); "Jesus, the mediator of a new covenant" (12:24) and so on. Westcott also draws attention to the fact that "in every case but 13:12, which is a simple historic statement, the name 'Jesus' occupies an emphatic position at the end of the clause."[18]

The author uses honorific titles which are common in the early tradition - Christ (9 times), Son (7 times, 2 of them in quotations of Ps 2:7), Lord (twice), the Son of God (3 times) - and his use of them is important; but, for his purpose in the treatise, what is of paramount importance is to remind his readers of Jesus, and of certain remembered facts about him, qualities he displayed and actions he did. Throughout, Jesus is pointed to as the Example, the Exemplar, to whom Christians must continually look, whose path they must continually follow. Hugh Anderson says that Hebrews "offers a stringent rebuttal to the attitude of those modern theologians who are reluctant to think of the Cross as a genuinely historical act issuing from the righteousness and obedience and moral perfection of Jesus, for fear of relapsing into the liberal view."[19] It is an equally strong rebuttal of those who hesitate to think of Jesus as the Example that Christians must follow, those who hesitate to think of "being a Christian" in terms of imitation of Christ. To be sure, "imitatio Christi" is not the whole of what it means to be a Christian, and there is more to the person and work of Christ than providing an example. But being a Christian involves discipleship, and discipleship means following,[20] and following Jesus is what the Letter to the Hebrews is all about.

The author of Hebrews uses "shockingly human terms" to describe Jesus in order to underline the reality and authenticity of Jesus' humanness, and it is this theme that all the others subserve. The new covenant is superior because Jesus the man is superior, and his superiority is a superiority which manifests itself in his manhood in and through which God brings "many sons to glory," that is, to the glory of full humanness. Even the picture of Jesus as the high priest who is mediator of the new covenant (9:15) is meant to underline his humanness and his power to lead his brethren into that same humanness of which he himself partook. "He who sanctifies and those who are sanctified have all one origin. That is why he is not ashamed to call them brethren ... Since therefore the children share in flesh and blood, he himself partook of the same nature ... He had to be made like his brethren in every respect so that he might become a merciful and faithful high priest in the service of God ... Because he himself has suffered and been tempted, he is able to help those who are tempted" (2:11-18). This point is made very clearly by Graham Hughes who says:

the significance of Jesus' life is expressed in more than one way: his identification with humanity appears to have been regarded as necessary for his defeating of the enemies of man (2:14f); distinguishable from this is the idea that Jesus' full experience of human life was necessary to qualify him as a "faithful and merciful" high priest, i.e. as one who understands the human predicament (2:17f). But beyond both of these is also the understanding that Jesus' endurance of humiliation represents a definitive pattern for the stance and attitude of the Christians who follow him. That this continuity of experience between Jesus and his disciples is the dominant concern in the reference here to Jesus' humanity is ensured by the fact that the real question to which the passage directs itself is that concerning the Christians' present "peirasmoi" (trials); that is to say, Jesus' steadfastness in humiliation (with its eventual outcome in vindication) is here introduced precisely as a response to the community's preoccupation with its particular afflictions.[21]

Hughes goes on to demonstrate the importance for the author of this "continuity of experience" between Jesus and his disciples, not simply those who followed him during the days of his earthly ministry, but also and more importantly those who are his disciples in the here and now of the author's own time.

The author points his readers to at least five specific features of Jesus' humanness which are of primary importance for their humanness, both as features to be imitated and as qualities which through Jesus will be generated in them:

(i) Firstly there is the emphasis on Jesus praying to God. "In the days of his flesh, Jesus offered up prayers and supplications, with loud cries and tears ... and he was heard for his godly fear" (5:7). The Greek of the last phrase, "apo tês eulabeias," is susceptible of a variety of interpretations. The word "eulabeia" occurs only here and at 12:28 and nowhere else in the New Testament. In 12:28 it is one of two words used to describe the attitude in which "acceptable worship" is to be offered. Here in 5:7 it implies submission to God's will in obedient acceptance. It is generally agreed that the primary reference is to the agony in Gethsemane (Mk 14:32-42) and pars), but it is unnecessary to limit it only to that. The attitude of prayerful submission and dependence on his Father was one which marked the whole life of Jesus, and not simply the moment of extreme crisis.

(ii) This leads us on automatically to the emphasis on Jesus' obedience. We have already noticed that this theme played an important part in the synoptic depiction of Jesus, as well as in Paul's use of the kenosis-hymn in Phil 2:6-11, and in the contrast between the disobedience of Adam and the obedience of Christ in Rom 5:18-21. Further, in I Peter, although the actual word "obedience" is not used, Jesus' willingness to suffer even to death is proffered as an example, although, as Anderson points out, "behind and before all genuine "imitatio Christi" is the "living hope" and resultant joy in suffering which have come to men through the Resurrection of Jesus Christ from the dead and by which he is most intimately present."[22] In Hebrews Jesus' obedient submission to God is expressed in the words of Isaiah 8:17-18 quoted in Heb 2:13 as words of "the pioneer of salvation" (2:10): "I will put my trust in him ... Here am I, and the children God has given me." Later, in the passage which we have seen to be primarily a reference to Gethsemane, we have the stark assertion that "although he was a Son, he learned obedience through what he suffered; and being made perfect he became the source of eternal salvation to all who obey him" (5:8-9). Having said negatively in 4:14 that Jesus was sinless ("in every respect tempted as we are, yet without sin"), now it is said positively that he learned obedience and was made perfect. Hebrews, like I Peter and Paul, makes the death on the cross the supreme demonstration of Jesus' obedience, but, as Eduard Schweizer emphasizes, behind this "there is a way of thinking which regards the whole earthly life of Jesus as an act of obedience which is above all completed in his shameful, humiliating passion."[23] That

Jesus "learned obedience" presupposes a truly human inner development. Indeed, as Cullman remarks, "The life of Jesus would not be really human if its course did not manifest a development."[24]

(iii) Closely linked with obedience is the fact that Jesus was tempted, "Because he himself has suffered and been tempted, he is able to help those who are tempted" (2:18); "We have not a high priest who is unable to sympathize with our weaknesses, but one who in every respect has been tempted as we are, yet without sin" (4:15). This memory of the fact that Jesus suffered temptation goes beyond what we find in the synoptic accounts which record the temptations which Jesus faced as Messiah, that is, the temptations which arose out of his consciousness of having been called to a mission and his desire to fulfil it; they were the temptations which James Denney describes in a sermon as "the wrong roads to the Kingdom."[25] But Hebrews emphasizes that Jesus was tempted in every respect as we are; he is thinking of the common temptations connected with our human weakness, the temptations to which we are exposed simply because we are men.

(iv) Jesus is human in the same way as all men: "Since the children share in flesh and blood, he himself likewise partook of the same nature" (2:14). "He had to be made like his brethren in every respect" (2:17) - that is basic to Hebrews' christology; and yet in one respect he was different - he was without sin (4:15) At two crucial points in his argument the author makes the blunt statement "it was fitting," an assertion that goes beyond rational or logical demonstration. "It was fitting that he [God], in bringing many sons to glory, should make the pioneer of their salvation perfect through suffering"(2:10) "it was fitting that we should have such a high priest, holy, blameless, unstained, separated from sinners, exalted above the heavens. He has no need, like those high priests, to offer sacrifices daily, first for their own sins and then for those of the people; he did this once for all when he offered up himself" (7:26f). Sinlessness cannot be proved; neither can perfection. Yet this manner in which Jesus is said to differ does not make him less than fully human; it makes him more genuinely human than any other man. Jesus is man as God intends him to be, and because he is this, he is able to lead us to share in that fullness of humanness which is his. "We share in Christ, if only we hold our first confidence firm to the end" (3:14).

(v) This leads us finally to an aspect of Jesus' humanness, as we encounter it in Hebrews, to which little attention has been paid in the history of christology. Undoubtedly passing reference to it can be found, but the idea of Jesus as having faith, as being a man of faith, has not been taken seriously until fairly recently. Thomas Aquinas' view that "from the first moment of his conception Christ had full vision of God in his essence ... Therefore he could not have had faith,"[26] probably expresses the unexpressed assumption of countless other theologians. How could the second person of the Trinity have faith? What need is there for faith where there is already the unclouded beatific vision?

While it is rarely said in the New Testament that Jesus had faith, it underlies and indeed is the foundation of all the other ways in which the humanness of Jesus is expressed - his praying, his obedience, his being tempted, his likeness to us in every respect except sin. Trustful dependence on the Father, the very awareness of being in the Father-Son relationship, characterizes Jesus in the Synoptics. It is implicit in Paul's witness to Christ and indeed may even be explicit if the genitive "Christou" in the phrase "pistis Christou" which occurs seven times in the Pauline corpus, is taken as subjective, that is, if the phrase is taken to mean Christ's faith.[27] It is in Hebrews, however, that the idea is most explicit. In the catena of Old Testament texts which the author uses to prove that Jesus is "not ashamed to call them brethren," he includes Isaiah 8:17, "I will put my trust in him"; like "his brethren," Jesus is one who lives by faith in God.

More important however is the description of Jesus in 12:2 as "the Pioneer and Perfecter of faith" which is almost universally mistranslated by the unwarranted insertion of "our" before "faith." Already in 2:10, Jesus has been described as "the pioneer of their salvation," while in 6:20-21 Jesus has been said to have entered "the inner shrine behind the curtain, where [he] has gone as a forerunner on our behalf." The description of Jesus as "the Pioneer and Perfecter of faith" (12:2) follows the long list of examples of faith in chapter 11, that is of those who, with countless others of whom "time would fail to tell" (11:32), now constitute "the great cloud of witnesses" by which "we are surrounded" (12:1). In view of this, the author exhorts his readers to perseverance in the race set before them, "looking to Jesus the Pioneer and Perfecter of faith." Earlier in the epistle

Jesus is "made perfect" (2:10ff; 5:7ff; 7:28) in his fulfilling "in a true human life the destiny of man personally" (Westcott[28]). He whose obedience is brought to perfection, or who perfects his faith, is also the one who originated faith as the pioneer (archêgos);he is the supreme paradigm of faith, summing up, in the faith manifested in his own life and death, the faith of all those who have lived by faith. Yet, at the same time, as the Pioneer, it is he who has made the following of his example of faith possible; he has blazed the trail for others to follow. R. H. Fuller draws attention to two analogies which may help us to understand the relationship between Christ's obedience and faith and ours: "C. S. Lewis once compared the situation to that of a child trying to make his first letters. The father puts his own large hand over the child's small hand and traces the letters with him. E. Schweizer compared the situation to an experience of his own childhood. In the alpine snow his father would walk ahead making footsteps in which the child could follow."[29]

We have stayed longer with Hebrews than we had intended, but it has been for good reasons. After almost total neglect, the christology of Hebrews is now receiving the attention it deserves in contemporary thinking about Jesus. Within the framework of the belief that the life and death and exaltation of Jesus are the work of God (i.e. of a christology-from-above), Hebrews concentrates attention on the humanness of Jesus in a way no other New Testament writing does. Yet is has nothing to say about how God is acting in the man Jesus. It does not speculate on the mode of "incarnation," a word I have avoided on purpose when speaking of Hebrews; it is concerned with him as a man, as the man, through whom God brings "many sons to glory" (2:10) by "sharing in him" (3:14).

It is, in fact, from the Fourth Gospel and the First Letter of John, writings which if not by the same hand certainly issue from the same "circle" (Cullmann) or "school" (Culpepper), that the idea of incarnation emerges, which was to become dominant in the development of the doctrine of the Person of Christ. Indeed it may be said that it was specifically the Prologue of the Gospel that laid down the pattern for future christological development. "In the beginning was the Logos, and the Logos was with God and the Logos was God ... and the Logos became flesh and dwelt among us, full of grace and truth ... No one has ever seen

God; the only Son [or, the only God], who is in the bosom of the Father, he has made him known" (John 1:1,14,18). This "christology-from-above," beginning with the eternal pre-existence of the Logos with God and as God, is of course, hinted at in the Prologue to Hebrews, and in a number of hymns, confessions or acclamations quoted by Paul, yet it is here that it becomes explicit, and it is here that at last we find a statement of the how of "incarnation," how God became man: "the Logos became flesh." (The virginal conception stories, peculiar to Matthew and Luke, utilize a completely different "mythology" with which we cannot deal here, except to say that I find it impossible to see how they can be harmonized with the idea of the incarnation of the eternally pre-existent Logos.)

As I have attempted to show elsewhere,[30] it was very largely on the basis of the Fourth Gospel that the church developed its doctrine of the "homoousion," the con-substantiality of the Father and the Son, but, in doing so, it found difficulty in maintaining in clear equipoise the humanity and the divinity of Jesus Christ. Despite the fact that the earliest heresy combatted by the church was docetism which denied the reality of the humanity of Jesus, the church was always in danger of failing to do the humanity justice. Further, despite the clearly anti-docetic emphasis of the Gospel and Letters of John it is possible that John himself did not completely avoid the danger, if Ernst Käsemann is right.[31] Whether the Jesus of John is fully human or does not quite become fully human, as Käsemann argues, depends ultimately on what John thinks "being human" is.

Among the masses of literature on the Fourth Gospel appearing during this century there are two books in particular which have influenced my thinking on the humanness of Jesus in the Fourth Gospel, and both have received little notice. Certainly both are now somewhat dated, yet both contain insights which are vital to a right understanding of John's Jesus. The first appeared in 1934, W. F. Lofthouse's "The Father and the Son,"[32] which may be seen partly as a protest against the age-old tendency of exegetes and theologians to treat the Logos-concept as the regulative concept in Johannine theology, and so to interpret the Gospel (and the whole Bible) in the light of the Prologue of John. Lofthouse argues that the Prologue "must be read after rather than before a close study of the Gospel."[33] He says that "into its eighteen verses the author has summoned all his leading and characteristic ideas. The recurring words are there, like the motifs of a symphony or an opera."[34] The Logos-concept, familiar in many different forms in the ancient world, is used to catch the readers' attention, and once that attention is caught, the concept is discarded in favour of the more personal concept "Son." Indeed Lofthouse goes so far as to say, "there is no Johannine doctrine of the Logos."[35] For Lofthouse, the regulative concept of the Gospel is "Son," and the Gospel is the Gospel of the Father-Son relationship: "We can only understand the Fatherhood of God when we study it in the light of the sonship of Jesus; when we watch the mutual activity of the two."[36] Further, Lofthouse argues that whereas in the rest of the New Testament the concept of sonship is more than peripheral but less than central, in the Johannine Gospel and Letters it is the main category for the contemplation of Jesus,[37] and it is to this literature more than any other that we owe the basis for the development of the specifically Christian doctrine of God as the Father of the Lord Jesus Christ. Thus the Fourth Gospel is to be seen as the development of sayings in the synoptic tradition of which the outstanding example is Matt 11:27 and as bringing to explicit expression the christology implicit in Jesus' use of "Abba" in address to God.

It is in John's Gospel that we find the paradox of the unity of the Father and the Son and the distinction between them. When the unity, expressed in sayings like, "He who has seen me has seen the Father" (Jn 14:9) and "I and the Father are one" (Jn 10:30), is taken as emphasizing the divinity of Jesus, it is frequently overlooked that his unity, which is basic to the doctrine of the Trinity, is one which also includes the mass of believers; in Jn 17:21f Jesus prays "that they all may be one; even as thou, Father, art in me, and I in thee, that they also may be in us ... that they may be one even as we are one, I in them and thou in me, that they may become perfectly one."

John makes no attempt to spell out the manner in which the Logos became flesh, but having asserted it, he proceeds to focus all attention on Jesus of Nazareth, who is this Logos-made-flesh, on his historical existence, his humanness, his relationship with God as Son with his Father, and his relationship with mankind. Whatever may be the distinction between the pre-existent Logos and God, John's concern is with the distinction between Jesus, the Son, and his Father. The Son does what he sees his Father doing (5:19), he can do nothing on his own authority (5:30), he speaks only as his Father taught him (8:28) or what he has seen with the Father (8:38), his food is to do the will of him who sent him (4:34). The distinction is best expressed in terms of obedience, dependence and faith, words which John never actually uses of Jesus, although it is certainly implied in Jn 15:10, "I have kept my Father's commandments, and abide in his love"; this dependence is even spoken of in terms of subordination: "The Father is greater than I" (14:28),[38] a text which caused considerable difficulty in the trinitarian controversies.

It is in the other neglected book that we find this dependence of the Son on the Father most clearly spelled out: J. Ernest Davey's, "The Jesus of St John," published in 1958.[39] A large part of this book is devoted to a study of "The Dependence of Christ as Presented in John" (pp.90-157), the thesis of which is stated in the previous chapter in these words: "The real Christ of the Fourth Gospel lives in absolute dependence at every moment upon the Father and in perfect harmony with his mind and purposes" (p.77). Davey proceeds to give an exhaustive list of the things for which Jesus depends on the Father in John, nineteen in all: power, knowledge, life, authority, guidance, message, and so on. This "dependence at every point" he traces to a historical basis as evidence for the reality of the humanness of Jesus, even though, like his old tutor, A. E. Brooke, and Ernst Käsemann he concludes that there is present in John a tendency to modify the history in the direction of docetism. The force of his argument about Jesus' dependence must be accepted, but it is possible that Raymond Brown is right when he argues that the tendency to relativize the humanity of Jesus is not the intention of the evangelist, but rather "how the gospel could have been read" by those who, according to the First Letter, had seceded from the Johannine community. Nonetheless Brown points out in a footnote, in a way that echoes what a number of other writers have pointed out, that the Johannine Jesus does seem to be less human than the Jesus of Hebrews. "The Johannine Jesus is not 'one who in every respect has been tempted as we are, yet without sinning' or 'one who has learned obedience through what he suffered, being made perfect' (Heb 4:15; 5:8-9). More adeptly than John, the Epistle to the Hebrews has kept in tension a high christology and full humanity."[40]

Yet once again we are forced back to the question what "being human" really means, and, as regards John's Jesus, Lofthouse again helps us. He says, in his chapter "Christ the Perfect Man," "Christ was really and truly man. He was a man, of course, living our human life, as much as John and Peter and Thomas his disciples. But he was man in a sense in which they were not; what they were imperfectly, he was in completeness ... If we could tolerate the paradox, we might say that he was man because he was what no man had ever been before."[41] In other words, rather than being less human than other men, Jesus is more human, for he is man as God intends him to be. To quote Lofthouse again, "Christ did not become what men were; he became what they were meant to be, and what they too, through accepting him, actually became."[42] Or to put it into the more existential language favoured by the contemporary christologians, he shows us what authentic humanness is, and at the same time opens for us the possibility that we too may participate in his authentic humanness,[43] the life which he knew in relationship with the Father, and which the Father in his love gives to all who trust in him (3:16).

This same-yet-different nature of Jesus' humanity is the beginning of the new creation of which Paul wrote, the beginning of the new revelation of which Hebrews speaks. John commences his gospel, "In the beginning ...." Here is the new genesis of man; here in Jesus of Nazareth the Logos becomes flesh; here in this Son who alone reveals the Father (1:18; 8:19; 14:7,9) is the new manhood, the humanness for which God made man, but which man, through disobedience and rebelliousness, has failed to attain. "What came to be in him was life, and the life was the light of men" (1:4). Through Jesus Christ, we can become children of God (1:13); apart from I Peter 1:3, as far as I can ascertain the language of "birth" and "begetting" is given a theological meaning only in John (in John "gennaô"; in I Peter "anagennaô"). The only time the word is used of Jesus is in Jesus' reply to Pilate (18:37), "For this I was born and for this I have come into the world," where it certainly refers to Jesus' physical birth. Jesus is described as "monogenes" which has no relation to begetting, but means "unique, only one of his kind." As the one in whom

God makes his new beginning with man, Jesus is unique, the Son; through trust in him we are begotten as children, and participate in the new humanness in which there is perfect freedom. "Eternal life" is God's gift here and now, a gift known in the fellowship of Jesus' disciples; the relationality which Jesus has with God is the paradigm of the relationality we have with him, with the Father, with each other. If there is any objection to John's teaching on the unity between God and man, which it is God's purpose and will to establish through his becoming man in Jesus, it may be that as Lofthouse says "it is, if anything, so rich and audacious as to frighten us by its refusal to stop short until it has placed us where Christ is, in the full blaze of the splendour of the Father's brightness, the unclouded intensity of his grace. If that is a fault the evangelist cannot be acquitted of it."[44]

The relationality which we have seen to have been the basic contribution of Judaism to the understanding of humanness, the I-Thou relationship between man and God, man and his fellowman, finds its perfect expression in Jesus, in the completeness of his relationship with his Father and in his utter self-giving for those who trust in him, indeed, if we take John 3:16 seriously, for the whole human race. Jesus, in the Johannine tradition, is the paradigm of humanness, the relationality with God and humanity which is characteristic of genuine humanness. This humanness, visible in Jesus, is the destiny of man, a destiny which John describes as "eternal life," into which, through faith in Jesus Christ, we are born as children of God (Jn 1:12-13). The author of the First Letter put it in a nutshell when he wrote (I Jn 3:2):

Beloved, we are God's children now; it does not yet appear what we shall be, but we know that when he appears we shall be like him, for we shall see him as he is.

Chapter VI

HUMANNESS IN CHRISTIAN TRADITION
AND CONTEMPORARY DEBATE

MY HOPE, in this final lecture with its somewhat grandiose title, is to to bring together some of the threads and tie up some of the loose ends of what I have been saying by leaping into the contemporary debate on humanness and humanization and seeking to assess some aspects of it. As I do this I shall have to drop in on some of the Early Fathers, for no discussion of christology can ignore the living insights which the Church has fossilized into the ecumenical creeds. When I chose my title and began preparing these lectures I had little idea of the vastness of the jungle I was attempting to penetrate; and if I have been able to make any penetration at all it has been only a narrow path in which I have tried to follow the voices of others in the forest and accept the help of their varied insights.

I have always had a strong interest in the humanness of Jesus and a dissatisfaction with scepticism both about the accessibility of Jesus of Nazareth through historical research and about the importance of the results of such research for Christian faith and for living out that faith today. The late Norman Perrin summed up the consensus of "historical facts" about Jesus achieved by the new quest in a single page, concluding with the words, "That, or something very like it, is all that we can know; it is enough."[1] But one may ask, "Enough for what?," or, as Patrick Henry asks, "How much history is enough?" "Identity as a Christian requires judgments about the significance of the historical date, judgments that must have some connection with the judgments made about Jesus by the apostles. It is clear that those early judgments were extraordinarily various, and nobody can claim <u>historical</u> justification for a narrow definition of Christianity."[2]

The intensive concentration on the historical questions about Jesus has tended to made us forget that there is a supra-historical dimension about the Christ-event without which Jesus would be no more than another figure in ancient history. The Jesus about whom questions are asked lives as the "Christus praesens" of the church's "Memory and Hope,"[3] from its very beginning to the present day. It is indeed this fact, the relationship between Jesus Christ and the community of faith that bears his name, that has raised so sharply in our generation the vital question, "Who is Jesus Christ?," with its no less important corollaries, "What is the Church?" and "What does it mean to be a Christian?"

Without detracting in any way from the attempts of Protestant theologians to answer the christological question, I must acknowledge that the importance of the issues involved has been brought home to me with the greatest force by recent Roman Catholic christological writing. My indebtedness to Roman Catholic writers should already be apparent from the frequent references I have already made to them. It is probably too early to give a diagnosis of the causes for this post-Vatican II outbreak of christological thinking, although a preliminary diagnosis may be helpful. Certainly, in view of the present hardening of conservatism in the Congregation for the Doctrine of Faith, with its "examination" of Schillebeeckx, Schoonenberg, Charles E. Curran, Leonardo Boff and others, and its condemnation of Hans Küng, the prognosis is not good.[4] But as for the diagnosis, the encyclical of Pope Pius XII, "Divino afflante Spiritu," in 1943, which Patrick Henry describes as "a bomb-burst,"[5] shattered the protective walls erected forty years earlier to guard against the perils of "modernism." The way was opened for a break-through in biblical (and patristic) scholarship which paved the way for the Second Vatican Council in the nineteen-sixties. The Council focused attention on the Church: its structure, its nature as "the people of God," its role in the modern world, its relationship to the so-called "separated brethren" and to people of non-Christian faiths. Out of the fresh understanding of what the Church is and should be, a new ecclesiology emerged. Yet the documents of Vatican II make no explicit statement on christology, which must be the basis of all Christian theologizing. As a result, Catholic theologians have found themselves forced to try to make explicit the christology which is implied in the new ecclesiology and in the new ecclesiastical stance in relation to the world. It is not that they no longer respect the classical formulations of Nicaea and Chalcedon, but, acknowledging the bipolarity of christological thinking, they are seeking to understand and to help the Church to understand "who Jesus Christ is for us today."

The church that emerged from Vatican II was still the divine-human institution of past doctrine, but now the emphasis was on the human dimensions of the church, the church as a human institution, or rather as a human community. The Dogmatic Constitution on the Church spoke of God's plan "to dignify men with a participation in his own divine life" (2), bringing about man's redemption by the obedience of his Son (3), who "in the human nature which he united to himself, redeemed man and transformed him into a new creation ... By communicating his Spirit to his brothers, called together from all peoples, Christ made them mystically into his own body" (7). So far it all sounds very traditional, but then it proceeds to speak of the church as "the people of God," and it is this theme of the human "peoplehood" of the church which dominates all the rest of the documents. The church, as "the people of God," exists in the world as a servant pilgrim people, whose task it is to be truly human, to realise the humanity for which God has created man, and to be the means of promoting "a more human way of life ... in this earthly society" (41).

The Dogmatic Constitution on Divine Revelation acknowledged the presence of the human element in the process of the formation, transmission and interpretation of Scripture; the decrees on the Ministry of Priests and Religious, and on the missionary activity of the church emphasized the servant role of the church in the world and of the ministry from highest to lowest as servants of the servant people of God; while the constitution on the liturgy brought the church's worship down to earth, humanizing it by enabling ordinary men and women to participate in it in the simplicity of their everyday speech.[6]

The human dimension of the church as the people of God, as the body of Christ in the world and in relation to the world, comes to most explicit expression in the Pastoral

Constitution on the Church in the World ("Gaudium et Spes"). Responding to the predicament of man today, threatened by dehumanization by technological, political and social developments, this document takes pains to spell out the dignity of the human person, very largely in biblical terms of creation in God's image and of God-given responsibilitiy for and dominion over the rest of the created order. Yet, at the same time, it emphasizes that man is made for interpersonal communion so that "unless he relates himself to others he can neither live nor develop his potential" (12), and that the root of man's dignity lies in his call to communion with God (19). It is in this setting that we have the most explicit christological statement of Vatican II in a brief paragraph on "Christ as the New Man" (22). Again the language is almost entirely biblical: Christ is the last Adam, the image of the invisible God, the perfect man (22). "By suffering for us he not only provided us with an example for our imitation, he blazed a trail, and if we follow it, life and death are made holy and take on a new meaning"(22). In the light of this doctrine of man and emphasis on the humanness of Jesus, the document goes on to speak about the societary nature of man's calling in God's plan, the interdependence of the individual person and society, reverence for the human person, equality and social justice, human solidarity, man's activity in the world, coming finally to the discussion of the Role of the Church in the Modern World and the Proper Development of Culture. The church is the people of God, called, redeemed, sanctified to be the transforming leaven in the lump of human society; through the humanness of the church as a community of human beings God works for the completion and perfection of the humanness of man, society, and culture in this world.

It is against this background that contemporary Roman Catholic christological discussion is taking place. The new ecclesiology has demanded a new look at christology and a re-assessment of the humanity of Jesus on the one hand, and, on the other, a re-examination of the Church's role in leading men and women to the achievement or attainment of the humanness for which God made them, of which Jesus Christ is the paradigm, and into which God, through Jesus Christ, redeems, saves, liberates them. This re-assessment and re-examination is leading in directions which the ecclesiastical authorities are finding extremely disconcerting. Openness to the Bible on the one hand and to the world on the other, are the poles from which the Church is trying to understand herself and her role, just as Jesus, the One attested by the Bible, and the concrete worldly situation of each community are the poles from which the church has always to formulate her christology. The new ecclesiology of Vatican II has demanded a re-thinking of christology of the kind which, as we saw earlier, Karl Rahner had foreshadowed in his programmatic essay of 1954, yet going far beyond anything Rahner could have imagined. A recent article by an American Jesuit says, "Christology is at the centre of Roman Catholic scholarly attention ... The attention given to the earthly life of Jesus ... is the fruit of the decades-long renewal of Catholic biblical scholarship. This new focus marks a striking departure from the older dogmatic tradition. At the same time, such fresh attention to the earthly career of Jesus necessarily reflects on the theologians' understanding of the symbol of faith bequeathed to us by Chalcedon."[7]

The critical nature of the human predicament lays upon the whole church the prophetic task of proclaiming God's Word of judgment and salvation here and now. Some may protest against the danger of letting the world set the agenda for the church for fear that this might imply that the world dictates to God. Yet, as I have emphasized a number of times, the concrete human situation in which the church is placed today is one of two poles, or one of two foci of the ellipse of the church's faith and praxis, and of the expression of that faith and praxis in her worship and life as the people of God. Schillebeeckx expresses it thus:

> The material content of the "Good News," the gospel and salvation, for us changes according to our experience of the absence of salvation. It is clear from the history of Christianity since the time of the early church that the material content of this Good News of salvation experienced in Jesus has been described in constantly changing forms, a process which is continuing for us.[8]

The result is that there is a new awareness of the necessity of "contextualization" of the gospel and of theology (to use that monstrous word which is so popular in contemporary discussion of missionary endeavour abroad and ministerial training at home!), and this interaction between theology and the religious, social, political, racial, cultural context in which theology is done can only result in pluralism, in a pluriformity of expression of the good news both in proclamation and theology - and, I may add, a pluriformity both of proclamation and of theology which reflects that of the New Testament and of the church ever since New Testament times.

There is almost complete unanimity that within the New Testament period there was a tremendous diversity of response to the Christ-event. Indeed James Dunn, probably with some exaggeration, argues that the church in the New Testament period was "more ecumenically diverse than it has been ever since."[9] I hope that this diversity has become evident in my discussion of the humanness of Jesus in the New Testament. It is acknowledged or simply tacitly presupposed by most contemporary christologians. Rahner's 1954 essay suggested the possibility of taking other strands of New Testament witness to Jesus as the starting point instead of those few texts traditionally used to support classical scholastic christology, while Wiles' more recent essay has made the same kind of suggestion. Wiles' point has been taken up by his fellow-contributors to "The Myth of God Incarnate"[10] who argue negatively about the adequacy of incarnation-talk, but, it seems to me, with one or two notable exceptions, to make little positive contribution, and the debate which has ensued has done little to rectify the situation.[11] When one compares the "Myth Debate" with the Catholic christological debate - Küng, Kasper, Schoonenberg, Schillebeeckx, Boff, Comblin, Gutierrez, Sobrino, van Beeck, Mackey, to mention only a few whose work has appeared in English - it is evident from which direction most light is coming at present. The latter are "experimenting" (to use Schillebeeckx's word) with New Testament models other than the Johannine which "from the Council of Nicaea onwards ... has been developed as a norm within very narrow limits and one direction ... in fact only this tradition has made history in the Christian churches."[12] Schillebeeckx calls for

a new and critical recall of pre-Nicene trends that will help to cancel out not the old choice but its one-sided emphasis and its silence regarding complementary but essential aspects. In that way a renewal of christology

94

will become possible within a new range of experience and new categories of understanding, in which definitive and final salvation in Jesus, imparted by God, is still encountered and still expressed.[12]

Having opened up the possibility of developing a christology for today from some model other than the Johannine-Nicene-Chalcedonian-Scholastic model, Catholic christologians are finding themselves on the horns of a dilemma. How can the "new christology" be harmonized with the Chalcedonian formula? In what sense is it possible, on the basis of the synoptic model or the Hebrews model or the Pauline model, to speak of "incarnation" in the usually accepted sense of the word? This point was raised by the Congregation for the Doctrine of Faith against Schille-beeckx's first volume, despite his vigorous assertion, "I have no trouble at all with any of this [the Council of Chalcedon],"[14] and that "the dogma of Chalcedon was the undisputed presupposition for me in the work of ... faith seeking historical understanding."[15] Whether he can maintain that position in the third volume remains to be seen.

The same criticism has been levelled, of course, at Hans Küng, despite his attempt, in the closing stages of his book, to emphasize his belief in the divine sonship of Jesus as the second person of the Trinity. Walter Kasper, who acknowledges the diversity of traditions of New Testament christology, takes Küng to task for tracing "the tradition back to the complexity of multiple and often contradictory traditions, and refusing to employ criteria "which help us to choose between THE Tradition and THE traditions."[16] That is, the question of the Tradition versus Scripture in its pre-Vatican II form is still being debated. The monitum of 1964 on "The Historical Truth of the Gospels," promulgated by the Pontifical Biblical Commission, not only gave biblical scholars the authority to apply all the historical critical methods to their study of scripture, but actually instructed them to do so, with the proviso that they should always be subject to the magisterium of the church. It is clear, however, that many are finding it difficult to face the possibility that this openness to scripture may demand of the church and its magisterium a reformulation of the traditional dogmas of what Catholics call "fundamental theology."[17] So Kasper and Rahner and others, while acknowledging "the multiple and often contradictory traditions" of scripture, still wish to make The Tradition determinative. (In much the same way, some Reformed Churches still in fact make the subordinate standard, e.g. the Westminster Confession, determinative of the sense in which ministers and office-bearers understand scripture!)

From another angle Kasper has criticized Küng, and at this point he is joined by Karl Rahner. This also brings us back to our main theme of humanness and humanization, and reveals the close parallel between Catholic criticism of Küng, Schillebeeckx and the liberation theologians, on the one hand, and, on the other, the "evangelical" criticism of the World Council of Churches' programme of humanization which we referred to in the opening lecture. In their responses to Küng's "On Being a Christian," both Kasper and Rahner seize on Küng's emphasis on salvation as "humanization" and his rhetorical question: "But does a reasonable man today want to be God?" with its implied negative answer which leads to the assertion: "our problem today is not the deification but the humanization of man."[18] Kasper declares that Küng thus "sets himself against the principle of the christology of the primitive church: 'God became man in order that man might become God.' "[19] For Kasper humanization means that being a Christian becomes something a man achieves for himself, and not something God does for him in Christ: "If the humanization of man becomes an alternative to his deification, we come dangerously close to Kant and to 'Religion within the Limits of Pure Reason.' "[20] Rahner also seizes on Küng's affirmation of humanization and asserts that his replacement of deification by humanization "has shocked me most of anything in the whole book."[21]

This criticism needs extremely careful examination, especially in view of the emphasis which so many are putting on salvation as humanization, and on the humanness of Jesus. It must also be examined in the light of Vatican II's repeated declarations about the "well-being" of man and "the need for a just society" in which man can realize the real humanness for which he was created, into which Christ has redeemed him, and towards the fullness of which the Holy Spirit makes him to grow. Kasper and Rahner assume that the idea of "deification" or "divinization" is fundamental to Christian faith. Kasper, as we have just seen, calls it "the principle of the christology of the early church as formulated in the much quoted statement: 'God became man that man might become God.' " and Küng himself calls it "a stirring patristic slogan."[22] Neither Kasper nor Rahner - nor even Küng himself - appears to have investigated the history of this idea in the early Fathers. Küng sees it as a patristic slogan which must be replaced, while Kasper and Rahner assume it to be a fundamental christological principle, by dismissing which Küng sells out the Gospel to subjectivism and secularization.

It is necessary and appropriate, then, that we should pause to ask just how fundamental the idea of deification is in the patristic tradition, and what exactly the Fathers who used it meant by the idea. Even a cursory reading of the article, "Divinisation," in "Le Dictionnaire de la Spiritualité"[23] shows that this language of deification played only a minor role in Eastern tradition: "it is met only in the Alexandrian tradition, slightly enlarged on by the Cappadocians ... Rather than use the non-scriptural term 'divinisation' the majority of authors prefer to speak of 'filiation' or 'regeneration.' "[24] It was of even less importance in the West: "the later Fathers of the Latin Church remain almost completely outside our scope; it is difficult to find any traces of the doctrine of deification with them."[25] The facileness with which de-ification is treated as a decisive principle of patristic theology arises, it seems, from a popular misunderstanding of patristic thought, a misunderstanding in which Protestant theologians also share. For example, Pannenberg makes the same general assumption: "The motif of deification determined, as is well known, the whole history of christology in the ancient church."[26]

Responsibility for introducing the concept into Christian tradition is usually laid at the door of Irenaeus (ca. 190 A.D.), although some would trace it back to Psalm 82:6: "I have said, You are gods," quoted by the Johannine Jesus in John 10:34, and to II Peter 1:4 which speaks of Christians as "partakers of the divine nature" (RSV), or as those "who come to share in the very being of God" (NEB). Ben Drewery has described the latter as "this fugitive phrase [in which] later theologians have found a treasure trove."[27] As far as Irenaeus is concerned the idea has to be read out of (or into!) the preface of "Against all Heresies," Book V: "Christ, out of his great love, became what we are, that he might make us what he is himself."[28] Elsewhere, and much more frequently, Irenaeus speaks in terms of the Son of God becoming man "so that man

... might become the son of God."[29] This language of filiation, of men becoming sons or children of God, which is common in the New Testament (e.g. Matt 5:45; Jn 1:12; Rom 8:14; Phil 2:15; Heb 2:10; I Jn 3:2), can hardly be interpreted to mean deification. Even Fathers like Athanasius, Gregory of Nazianzus and Augustine, who make the terse deification statement, "The Logos became flesh [or man] that we might become God [or be deified],"[30] also speak much more frequently in terms of adoption or filiation. Augustine, for example, says, "The only Son of God became a Son of man to make many sons of God";[31] or Leo the Great, in a Christmas sermon: "Christ ... became a son of man precisely in order that men could become sons of God."[32]

Look more closely at what the Alexandrian and Cappadocian traditions have to say. Even when Athanasius speaks of "deification," as he does in "De Incarnatione," 54, he is referring to the restoration to sinful man of that which, as man, he had lost at the Fall. Through the Christ-event (incarnation and atonement), man, who had ceased to participate in the Logos because of the Fall (i.e. he had become "alogos"), participates once more in the Logos (i.e. he becomes "logikos" again). For Athenasius, then, through the incarnation and atonement man is enabled by God to become what God had originally made him to be, namely a fully human being.[33] This leads to an apparently paradoxical conclusion: when Athanasius speaks of "deification," he means "humanization." If this is true of Athanasius, it is true also, but in a different way, of Gregory of Nazianzus who makes deification ("theosis") the centre of his theological enterprise. D. F. Winslow has recently shown, in the first study of Gregory's theology in English,[34] that for Gregory deification is not a restoration of man to a pristine state of perfection, but rather the realization of the potentiality, the destiny, for which God made man. So Gregory thinks of deification as dynamic growth towards our ultimate destiny.[35] "Theosis" was the created destiny of man; "theosis" is our recreated destiny.[36] "Our created vocation of progressing towards 'theosis' does not do away with our creatureliness; rather it fulfils it. For one to be 'deified' is to be a 'creature' of God, as God intended one to be. 'Theosis,' as Gregory once said,[37] cannot be taken 'literally'; one cannot literally 'become God' since that would be as absurd as if we were to state that God is a 'creature'."[38] Winslow shows that in describing salvation as "theosis," Gregory uses the word not literally but as a metaphor - spatial, visual, epistemological, ethical, corporate and social[39] - to describe "a relation between God and creation, not a definition either of us or of God separate from one another," a relation which is not static but dynamic: "We were created to grow into an increasingly intimate relation with God."[40] For Gregory deification is the process by which God enables man to become what God created him to be, fully and authentically human in relationship with God and with his fellow-men.

In the light of this brief examination of what some of the Fathers who used deification-talk meant by it, Küng's emphasis on humanization should not be so shocking after all. In Jesus Christ God became human so that man might become fully human. The humanness of Jesus, which is the humanness or humanity of God, is paradigmatic and creative of our humanness. For the Fathers, fullness of the humanness of Jesus was necessary for the fullness of man's salvation. For Küng the humanization of man depends on and is derived from the creative and re-creative humanity of God who encounters us in the man Jesus.[41] I have not argued this point in defence of Küng; I have done it in order to indicate how, in the area we have been concerned with in these lectures, in contemporary debate the idea of humanization has been falsely seen as the opposite of what the Fathers meant by deification by attributing to the latter a meaning which, in fact, is warranted neither by scripture nor by patristic tradition.

Emphasis on salvation as humanization is central both in contemporary Protestant missiology and in contemporary "political" or "liberation" theologies, most of which come out of Latin American Roman Catholicism.[42] The humanness of Jesus, the one who identified himself with the poor and the oppressed and the outcasts and stood with them and for them against political and religious authorities, proclaiming liberation to the captives and good news to the poor, the one who himself suffered degradation and death at the hands of the rulers of this world - the humanness of this Jesus has become the focal point of faith and hope and love for those on whom has been laid the task of proclaiming and making effective the liberating power of the love of God manifested for us men and our humanization in the very humanness of Jesus.

The theologians who genuinely seek to enunciate a "christology-from-below," taking the humanness of Jesus as their starting point, see their work, not as a radical departure from classical christology, to which they affirm their allegiance, but rather as an attempt to find alternative ways of expressing that faith which are more appropriate for mankind in its predicament at the end of the twentieth century. Like the Antiochene theologians of old, however, having started from the humanness of Jesus, they have difficulty in finding appropriate language with which to affirm the "divinity" of Jesus. Certainly the ascription of "divinity" to this particular man, Jesus of Nazareth, can only be made in faith; it is not rationally, scientifically or historically demonstrable. The classical christology begins with the leap of faith: the Word, which was in the beginning with God and was God, became flesh, and we beheld his glory. But if we start our christology from below, from the man Jesus, as his first followers did, then, like them, we are led to the point where we too are confronted with the question of Jesus, "Who do you say I am?" The mystery of Jesus' humanness, his total abandonment on the Cross, demand of us the response of faith: "You are the Christ," or, in John's version, "You are God's holy one, and we have known and believed that you have the words of eternal life." Confronted with the mystery of Jesus, we too are led to doxology and acclamation, to acknowledge Jesus as Lord and to acknowledge that it is in him that we find God himself encountering us as the one who recreates us so that the possibilities of real and full humanness which we see in Jesus may indeed be ours in relationship with God the Father and with all his children of mankind.

NOTES
INDEXES

NOTES

NOTES TO CHAPTER I

Introduction: The Human Predicament

1   SCM, London, 1953, p.9

2   Or should "Cur Deus Homo?" be translated "Why the God-Man?"?

3   The title of a treatise by Innocent III.

4   "In our Image and Likeness": Humanity and Divinity in Italian Humanist Thought, 2 vols., Constable, London, 1970.

5   Ibid. vol. I, p.180.

6   Williams & Norgate, London, 1904.

7   Gaudium et Spes, para.3.

8   Ibid., para.55. On this aspect of Vatican II see Joseph J. Spae, East Challenges West - Towards a Convergence of Spiritualities, The Charles Strong Memorial Trust, Melbourne, 1979, p.76.

9   E. Bloch, Das Prinzip Hoffnung, 1959.

10   See, for example, June Goodfield, On Playing God, Hutchinson, London, 1977.

11   International Review of Mission, vol.60 (1971).

12   Ibid.,

13   Humanisierung: Einzige Hoffnung der Welt?, MBK Verlag, Bad Salzuflen, p.56; quoted in English translation by M. M. Thomas, "Salvation and Humanization," in: International Review of Mission, vol.60 (1971), pp.28f.

14   "Mission and Humanization," in: International Review of Mission, vol.60 (1971), p.22.

15   The Uppsala '68 Report, WCC, Geneva, 1968, Sect.II.

16   Art. cit., p.18.

17   Phrases borrowed from Joseph Spae (see note 8 above). Krister Stendahl has demonstrated that the individualistic emphasis in Western Christianity has its origin, not in Scripture but in the introspectiveness of Augustine: see "St Paul and the Introspective Conscience of the West" in: Paul among Jews and Gentiles, Fortress, Philadelphia, 1976.

18   "Salvation and Humanization," in: International Review of Mission, vol.60 (1970), p.29.

19   The "terrorist" guerilla war in Zimbabwe-Rhodesia, so frequently deplored by the western powers as Marxist-inspired, and the subject of such heated contoversy in some of the member Churches of the W.C.C., has been shown by the recent elections to have been the only way in which more than ninety per cent of black Rhodesians could gain for themselves the basic human right of self-determination.

20   This has been highlighted by the death of Archbishop Romero in San Salvador, who, after supporting the junta which overthrew the military regime of his namesake, Colonel Romero, became an outspoken critic of the new regime: "They have used repressive violence, producing a greater number of dead and wounded than the old military regime" (Article by Peter Deeley in: "The Otago Daily Times," Dunedin, April 9, 1980, p.3.).

21   A quotation from T. S. Eliot, "Choruses from 'The Rock'," III, lines 35-36.

22   Creation and New Creation: The Past, Present, and Future of God's Creative Activity, Augsburg, Mineapolis, 1973, p.9.

23   Pope John Paul II, Redemptor Hominis, 15: "What modern man is afraid of."

24   See R. S. Franks, A History of the Doctrine of the Work of Christ, Hodder & Stoughton, London (n.d.).

25   H. Anderson (ed.), Jesus, Prentice-Hall, New York, 1967, p.16.

26   Walter Kasper, Burns & Oates, London, 1976.

27   W. Pannenberg, SCM, London, 1968.

28   John McIntyre, SCM, London, 1966.

29   Peter de Rosa, Collins, London, 1975.

30   Leonardo Boff, Orbis, New York, 1978.

31   E. Schillebeeckx, Collins, London, 1979.

32   Jon Sobrino, SCM, London, 1978.

33   James Mackey, SCM, London, 1979.

34   J. Hick (ed.), SCM, London, 1978.

35   F. E. Crowe in: Theological Studies, vol.29 (1968), 87-101.

36   W. Hamilton, quoted (without a reference) by F. E. Crowe, art. cit.

37   The Crucified God, SCM, London, 1974, p.92.

38   Ibid., p.93.   39   Ibid., p.125.

40   Ibid., p.4.   41   Ibid., p.93.
42   Jesus-God and Man, SCM, London, 1968, p.35.
43   Ibid., p.49.
44   Ibid., title of Part I, Ch.3, pp.53 ff.
45   Ibid., Part 1, Ch.4, pp.115ff.
46   Ibid., title of Part III, pp.191ff.
47   Jesus the Christ, Burns and Oates, London, 1976, p.37.
48   See J. D. G. Dunn, Unity and Diversity in the New
Testament, SCM, London, 1977.
49   Jesus Christ Liberator, Orbis, New York, 1978,
Chs.1-2. The same point is clearly made by Schillebeeckx who
says, "Through the movement brought to life by Jesus we are
confronted here and now with Jesus of Nazareth" (op. cit.
p.19, underlining mine), and a little later, "the basic
affirmation of the Christian creed is our confession
concerning Jesus, that is, 'Jesus of Nazareth,' that he is 'the
Christ, the only-begotten Son, our Lord. The fully normative
factor here is: 'credo in Jesum': I believe in the manifestation
of this quite concrete person, 'Jesus,' who appeared in our
history with the historical name 'Jesus of Nazareth.' In him
we find salvation, well-being. This is the fundamental creed
of primitive Christianity." (Ibid., p.23.)

NOTES TO CHAPTER II

Humanness in the Old Testament

1   "What Makes a Missionary?," in: G. H. Anderson and T.
F. Stransky (eds.), Mission Trends, No. 2, Paulist Press and
Eerdmans, Grand Rapids, p.123.
2   Theology of the Old Testament, Oliver & Boyd,
Edinburgh, 1962-66.
3   See G. E. Wright, God who Acts: Biblical Theology as
Recital, SCM, London, 1952. The main passages where we
encounter this recital of God's redemption of his people from
Egypt are Pss 78, 105, 106, 136; Deut 26:6ff; Josh 24; Neh 9.
It also occurs in Judith 5 and Stephen's speech in Acts 7 also
falls into the same category.
4   E.g. ("the God of the Fathers") - Deut 26-7; I Chron
12:17; 29:18; Ezra 7:27; et al.; see also Tobit 8:5; Judith 7:28;
10:8; Wisd 9:1; Dan 3:3 etc.; ("the God of Abraham ...") - Ps
47:9; Ex 3:6,15,16 etc.

5   Anthropology of the Old Testament, SCM, London, 1974, p.88.
6   See especially the caution expressed by J. W. Rogerson, "The Hebrew Conception of Corporate Personality: A Re-Examination," in: Journal of Theological Studies, n.s. vol.21 (1970), 1-16; and his book, Anthropology and the Old Testament, Blackwell, Oxford, 1978, pp.55-59.
7   Albert Gelin, The Concept of Man in the Bible, Geoffrey Chapman, London, 1968, p.60.
8   Quoted by Gelin, op. cit., p.60.
9   Wolff, op. cit., p.216.
10   Op. cit., pp.62f.   11   Wolff, op. cit., p.222.
12   For much of the foregoing I acknowledge my indebtedness to Piet Schoonenberg, Covenant and Creation, Sheed & Ward, London, 1968, pp.14ff.
13   Wolff, op. cit., p.221.
14   See E. P. Sanders, Paul and Palestinian Judaism, SCM, London, 1977.
15   See Victor P. Furnish, The Love Command in the New Testament, Abingdon, Nashville, 1972.
16   E. Schweizer, "Resurrection - Fact or Illusion?" in: Horizons in Biblical Theology, vol.1 (1979), p.139.
17   B. W. Anderson, Creation versus Chaos, Association Press, New York, 1967, p.35.
18   Ibid., p.38.
19   Creation, SPCK, London, 1971, p.26.
20   Idem.   21   Idem.
22   Ibid., p.19.   23   Op. cit., p.95.
24   "The Image of God in the Book of Genesis - a Study in Terminology," in: Bulletin of the John Rylands Library, vol.51 (1968), p.14.
25   N. H. Snaith, "The Image of God," in: The Expository Times, vol.91 (1979), p.20.
26   Op. cit., p.226.
27   John Reumann, op. cit., p.75.
28   Ibid., p.76.
29   The Relevance of Science, Collins, London, 1964, p.51. This same point is made very clearly by Rabbi David Neiman of Boston in his article, "The Polemic Language of the Genesis Cosmology," in: D. Neiman and M. Schatkin (eds.), The Heritage of the Early Church: Essays in Honour of Georges Vasilievich Florovsky, Pont. Inst. Studiorum Orientalium, Rome, 1973, pp.47-63.

30   SCM, London, 1956, pp.28f.
31   J. Reumann, op. cit., p.78.
32   Ibid., pp.79ff.
33   Reumann, op. cit., p.79; cf. also ibid., note 39, pp.122-123.
34   See J. Murphy-O'Connor, "Christological Anthropology in Phil II:6-11," in: Revue Biblique, vol.83 (1976), pp.31ff. I recall hearingMatthew Black on one occasion suggesting that in fact the Book of Daniel is a midrash on the Servant Songs, although he admitted that he was using "midrash" in a loose sense.
35   Wisdom in Israel, SCM, London, 1972, p.309.
36   Ibid., p.308.   37   Ibid., p.58.
38   Ibid., p.315.   39   Ibid., p.308.
40   Here I use for the first time a word which plays a role in Jon Sobrino's christology as we shall see later. See J. Sobrino, Christology at the Crossroads, SCM, London, 1978, p.331.

NOTES TO CHAPTER III

Jesus and Humanness in the Synoptic Tradition

1   R. Bultmann, Jesus and the Word, Nicholson & Watson, London, 1935, p.11. See also José Comblin, Jesus of Nazareth: Meditations on His Humanity, Orbis, New York, 1976, p.4: "Nevertheless, with all this filtration and all these elaborations of the details and the words, the person of Jesus, his human personality and presence shine forth with such a force that a true picture of him is unmistakable."
2   O.U.P., New York, 1964.
3   Ibid., p.147.
4   English translation in: Theological Investigations, vol.I, Darton, Longman & Todd, London, 1961, pp.149-200.
5   Ibid., p.168. It is interesting that the categories which Rahner lists are drawn mainly from John's Gospel (except, of course, Jesus' knowledge of the Father, cf. Mt 11:27), which is also the basic source and inspiration of the classical scholastical (incarnational) christology which Rahner is criticizing.
6   First published in: Religious Studies, vol.VI (1970),

pp.69-76, then reprinted in: S. W. Sykes and J. P. Clayton (eds.), Christ Faith and History, CUP, 1972, pp.1-12, and more recently in: Explorations in Theology, 4, SCM, London, 1979.

7   The Shape of Christology, SCM, London, 1966, p.136.

8   On Being a Christian, Collins, 1977, CI: "The Social Context," pp.177-213.

9   Ibid., p.205.

10   W. Barclay, The New Testament, Collins, London, 1968, vol.I, at Mk 2:15 and elsewhere.

11   In his Ferrie Lecture in Sydney in 1978, John McIntyre pointed out how central this theme has been in Scottish theology during the past century, particularly in writers like J. McLeod Campbell, James Denney and H. R. Mackintosh.

12   Op. cit., p.173.   13   Ibid., p.174.

14   James A. Sanders, "From Isaiah 61 to Luke 4," in: Jacob Neusner (ed.), Christianity, Judaism and other Greco-Roman Cults: Studies for Morton Smith, E. J. Brill, Leiden, 1975, vol.I, pp.75-106. For an interesting use of Sanders' point, see Robert Jewett, Jesus against the Rapture: Seven Unexpected Prophecies, Westminster, Philadelphia, 1979. Ch.III.

15   See my "Martyrdom and Resurrection in the New Testament," in: Bulletin of the John Rylands Library, vol.55 (1972), 240-51.

16   Jesus of Nazareth: Meditations on His Humanity, Orbis, Mary Knoll, New York, 1976, pp.153-57.

17   Op. cit., pp.320, 335.

18   Op. cit., p.171 (underlining mine).

19   To use Hans Küng's terminology.

20   Jesus-God and Man, p.369; see also pp.49, 159, 183, 195-8.

21   See ibid., pp.195ff. See also H. Heppe, Reformed Dogmatics, George Allen & Unwin, London, 1950, pp.458ff.

22   Op. cit., p.171.

23   The Teaching of Jesus, CUP (2nd edn. rep.) 1943, ch.IV.

24   J. Jeremias, The Central Message of the New Testament, SCM, London, 1965, ch.I; The Prayers of Jesus, SCM, London, 1967; New Testament Theology: vol.I: The Proclamation of Jesus, SCM, London, 1971, pp.36ff, 61ff.

25   See J. Sobrino, Christology at the Crossroads, passim; H. Küng, op. cit., pp.324ff et al.; J. Moltmann, The Crucified God, SCM, London, 1973, p.158; W. Kasper, Jesus the Christ,

passim; J. A. T. Robinson, The Human Face of God, SCM, London, 1973, passim.

26   The Central Message of the New Testament, p.22f.

27   Op. cit., p.108.

28   Promise and Fulfilment, SCM, London, 1957, p.41. The words quoted are a summary of Kümmel's view by H. Anderson, Jesus and Christian Origins, p.157.

29   "Knowledge in the Dead Sea Scrolls and Matthew 11:25-30," in: Christian Origins and Judaism, Philadelphia, 1962, pp.119ff. See also H. Anderson, op. cit., pp.157f.

30   Central Message," p.25. On the way in which Jesus "understood himself to stand in a unique relation of sonship to God" see R. H. Fuller, The Foundations of New Testament Christology, SCM, London, 1965, ch.V: "The Historical Jesus: His Self-understanding."

31   Op. cit., p.147.   32   Op. cit., p.34.

33   Jesus in the Gospels, Prentice-Hall, Englewood Cliffs, 1967.

34   Op. cit., p.384-9 et al.

35   Op. cit., p.104-11.

36   Op. cit., p.106 (see n.24 above).

37   Ibid.

38   New Testament Theology, pp.35f.

39   Words and phrases taken from H. Küng, op. cit., pp.211f, but echoed by a host of other writers.

40   E. Schweizer heads chapter 2 of his book, Jesus (London, 1971, p.13): "The Man who fits no formula."

41   What are they saying about Jesus?, Paulist, New York, 1977, p.39.

42   Ibid., p.37.

43   Jesus - God and Man, p.350.

44   Ibid., p.229.   45   Ibid., p.278.

46   Ibid., p.358.   47   Ibid., p.356.

48   It is interesting to note that at the end of his discussion of the 7th and 8th century Monothelite-Dyothelite debate H. R. Mackintosh wrote: "Thus by degrees the Church's memories of the human life of Jesus faded into oblivion. Men lost the sense of history" (The Doctrine of the Person of Jesus Christ, 2nd edn., Edinburgh, 1913, p.222).

49   New Testament Theology, pp.29ff.

50   Ibid., p.68.

51   G. O'Collins, op. cit., p.40.

52   Jesus the Christ, p.120.

53   The above is a summary of Kasper's own words on page 120.

54   The Aims of Jesus, SCM, London, 1979.

55   New Testament Theology, pp.276-299.

56   Nothing of Schürmann's work, of which Kasper and O'Collins also make frequent mention, has appeared in English. See Meyer, op. cit., p.310, note 124.

57   Op. cit., p.217.

58   Luke 22:43 is probably a later addition to the text of Luke, as this verse is omitted by many manuscripts.

59   On Being a Christian, p.340.

60   J. Sobrino, Christology at the Crossroads, SCM, London, 1979, p.185.

61   Idem.   62   Ibid., p.187.

63   Ibid., p.191-2.   64   Ibid., p.218.

NOTES TO CHAPTER IV

Humanness in the Early Preaching and Paul

3   See Lecture I, note 14.

2   See Lecture I, note 19.

3   Jesus the Christ, p.18.

4   Glaubhaft ist nur Liebe, Einsledeln, 1963; see Kasper, op. cit., p.25, note 13.

5   See H. Küng, On Being a Christian, p.388: "These names were not a priori intelligible means of identification, but pointers in his direction. They were not a priori infallible definitions, but a posteriori explanations of what he is and what he signifies." See also the excellent discussions in: Kasper, op. cit., pp.104ff; J. P. Mackey, Jesus - the Man and the Myth, SCM, London, 1979, pp.196ff; and of course F. Hahn, The Titles of Jesus in Christology, London, 1969.

6   Op. cit., p.343.   7   Ibid., p.344.

8   Ibid., p.348.

9   Ben F. Meyer, The Aims of Jesus, p.178.

10   Ibid., p.176-7.

11   Johannes Feiner and Lukas Vischer (eds.), The Common Catechism: A Christian Book of Faith", Search Press, London, 1975, p.163.

12   See A. Schweitzer, The Quest of the Historical Jesus,

Eng. trans., Black, London, 2nd edn., 1922, p.237, quoted by Meyer, op. cit., p.177; N. A. Dahl, The Crucified Messiah and Other Essays, Augsburg, Minneapolis, 1974, pp.25ff.

13 See my "Martyrdom and Resurrection in the New Testament," in: Bulletin of the John Rylands Library, vol.55 (1972) pp.240-51.

14 Op. cit., p.177.

15 This is especially true of the third prediction recorded by Mark (10:33); "Behold, we are going up to Jerusalem; and the Son of man will be delivered to the chief priest and the scribes, and they will condemn him to death, and deliver him to the Gentiles; and they will mock him and spit upon him and scourge him, and kill him; and after three days he will rise."

16 M. Hengel, The Son of God, SCM, London, 1976, p.2.

17 G. N. Stanton, Jesus of Nazareth in the New Testament Preaching, (S.N.T.S. Monograph 27), C.U.P. Cambridge, 1974.

18 Ibid., p.85.

19 See my "The Body of the Resurrection," in: Colloquium, vol.2 (1967) pp.105-115.

20 James Denney, Jesus and the Gospel, Hodder & Stoughton, London, 2nd edn., 1909, p.146.

21 D. M. Baillie, God Was in Christ, Faber & Faber, London, 2nd edn., 1955, p.97.

22 Ibid., pp.151f.

23 Church Dogmatics, IV: I, T. & T. Clark, Edinburgh, 1956, pp.48-53.

24 See Johannes Munck, Paul and the Salvation of Mankind, SCM, London, 1958, ch.I.

25 C. Kannengiesser, Foi en la Résurrection: Résurrection de la Foi, (Le Point Théologique, 9), Beauchesne, Paris, 1974, p.150.

26 See G. N. Stanton, op. cit., ch.4, for a discussion of these issues.

27 Jerome Murphy-O'Connor, Becoming Human Together, Michael Glazier Inc., Wilmington, 1977, pp.35-37.

28 See G. N. Stanton, op. cit., pp.110ff.

29 J. Murphy-O'Connor, Becoming Human Together (see note 27 above); "Christological Anthropology in Phil II, 6-11," in: Revue Biblique, vol.83 (1976), pp.25-50; "I Cor VIII,6: Cosmology or Soteriology?" in: Revue Biblique, vol.85 (1978), pp.253-267.

30 Murphy-O'Connor, Becoming Human Together, pp.42ff.

31   Paul and Rabbinic Judaism, SPCK, London, 1948, ch.3.

32   From First Adam to Last, A. & C. Black, London, 1962.

33   The Last Adam, Blackwell, Oxford, 1966.

34   Murphy-O'Connor, Becoming Human Together, p.44.

35   Ibid. pp.45-6.   36   Ibid., p.47.

37   Op. cit., p.48. G. P. Klubertanz, Introduction to the Philosophy of Being, p.153, says: "An intelligent agent engaged in the production of something has a more or less perfect knowledge of the thing he intends to make and directs his activity according to that knowledge. The object as known, according to which he directs activity, is called an 'exemplar'." Thomas Aquinas defines exemplar cause as 'a form (idea) in imitation of which something comes into being from the intention of the agent that determines its end for itself' (de Veritate, Q.3, A.1).

38   Op. cit., p.48.

39   I have developed this line of argument about the Colossian hymn in a paper read at the Annual Meeting of S.N.T.S. at Toronto in August, 1980, now published in: New Testament Studies, 27 (1981), pp.572-5.

40   "Christological Anthropology in Phil II, 6-11" p.49. See note 29 above.

41   Ibid., pp.49-50.

42   Zur Gedankenführung in den paulinischen Briefen, in: Studia Paulina [de Zwaan Festschrift], Haarlem, 1953, pp.152ff; "Zu Phil:2:7," in: Novum Testamentum, vol.6 (1963), pp.186f. See following note.

43   Art. cit., pp.26ff.

44   Crucifixion, SCM, London.

45   See my "The Integrity of Philippians," in: New Testament Studies, vol. 13 (1966) pp.57, 66.

46   C. F. D. Moule, The Origin of Christology, CUP, Cambridge.

NOTES TO CHAPTER V

Humanness in Hebrews and John

1   SCM, London, 1971 (Eng. trans. by David E. Green from the German: Jesus Christus, Siebenstern Verlag, Munich, 1968).

2   Ibid., ch.2.   3   Ibid., p.189.
4   See especially J. D. G. Dunn, Unity and Diversity in the New Testament, SCM, London, 1977. I have dealt with the christological aspect of this question of unity and diversity in "The Crisis of New Testament Theology," in: Religious Studies in the Pacific, (Papers read at a Theological Colloquium in Auckland, August 1977), Auckland University Press.
5   Christology at the Crossroads, pp.5, 13.
6   See his book of this title.
7   See again J. D. G. Dunn, Unity and Diversity in the New Testament, in this connection, especially ch.10.
8   Geoffrey Chapman, London, 1979.
9.   "The Old Testament in Hebrews," in: W. Klassen and G. F. Snyder (eds.), Current Issues in New Testament Interpretation, SCM, London, 1962, p.58.
10   E.g., B. F. Westcott, The Epistle to the Hebrews, Macmillan, London, 3rd edn. 1903, p.428; J. P. Alexander, A Priest For Ever, James Clarke & Co., London, 1937, p.92; H. Anderson, Jesus and Christian Origins, pp.283ff; R. Bultmann, History of the Synoptic Tradition, Blackwell, Oxford, 1963, p.303; et al.
11   The Christology of the New Testament, SCM, London 1959, p.93.
12   It is difficult to decide whether the apostasy has already happened or whether the author, seeing the possibility of it, warns his readers of the dangers towards which they are heading.
13   "Palestinian and Hellenistic Christianity: Some Critical Comments," in: New Testament Studies, vol.19 (1972/73), pp.271-87.
14   Judaism and Hellenism, Fortress, Philadelphia, vol.I, 1974. The implications are worked out in his smaller books: The Son of God, SCM, London, 1976; Acts and the History of Earliest Christianity, SCM, London, 1979.
15   It is still a presupposition of much German New Testament scholarship, and still dominates much non-German scholarship which allows itself to be overawed by the heavy artillery of the history-of-religions school.
16   See W. L. Knox, "The 'Divine Hero' Christology in the New Testament," in: Harvard Theological Review, vol.41 (1948), p.234: "the writer of Hebrews after opening with the emphatic statement that Jesus really is the Wisdom-Logos of

Pauline christology, and as such superior to the angels, leaves the whole of this conception on one side, and passes over to his character as the messianic Son of Man .... The writer thus avoids the difficulty of harmonizing the two conceptions and passes over to an exposition of the person of Christ in terms of a saviour from heaven who saves mankind by suffering."

17   The Epistle to the Hebrews, Macmillan, London, 3rd edn., 1903, pp.33f.

18   Idem.

19   H. Anderson, op. cit., p.282.

20   See especially E. Schweizer, Lordship and Discipleship, SCM, London, 1960.

21   "Hebrews and Revelation," Cambridge University Ph.D. Dissertation, pp.135f. This disseration has been published in a completely revised version under the title, Hebrews and Hermenuetics, (SNTS Monograph Series 36), CUP, Cambridge, 1980. The passage quoted above appears to have been revised out of the published version.

22   Op. cit., p.280.   23   Op. cit., pp.72f.

24   Christology of the New Testament, p.97.

25   James Denney, The Way Everlasting, Hodder & Stoughton, London, 1911, pp.189ff.

26   Summa Theologiae, III, q.7, a.3, quoted by Sobrino, op. cit., p.80.

27   See G. Howard, "On the 'Faith of Christ'," in: Harvard Theological Review, vol.60 (1976), pp.459-465.

28   Op. cit., p.67.

29   Commentary on Hebrews in: G. Krodel (ed.), Hebrews, James, I and II Peter Jude, Revelation, (Proclamation Commentaries), Fortress, Philadelphia, 1977, p.18. The reference to E. Schweizer is to: Lordship and Discipleship, SCM, London, 1960, p.11.

30   Johannine Christology and the Early Church, CUP, Cambridge, 1970.

31   So E. Käsemann, The Testament of Jesus, SCM, London, 1968. Käsemann is by no means the first to suggest that there is a strong docetic tendency in John. J. Ernest Davey (see note 37) recalls A. E. Brooke remarking that in John we seem (at first sight at least) to be presented with a picture of a god or "demi-god stalking through life" (p.12). See also R. E. Brown, The Community of the Beloved Disciple, Geoffrey Chapman, London, 1979, p.116.

32   SCM, London, 1934.   33   Ibid., p.46.

34   Ibid., pp.45-6.   35   Ibid., p.64.
36   Ibid., pp.40-41.   37   Ibid., p.63.
38   See C. K. Barrett, " 'The Father is greater than I': Subordinationist Christology in the New Testament," in: J. Gnilka (ed.), Neues Testament und die Kirche, Freiburg-Basel-Wien, 1974.
39   Lutterworth, London.
40   R. E. Brown, op. cit., p.116, n.230.
41   Op. cit., p.115.   42   Ibid., p.118.
43   See José Comblin, Sent from the Father: Meditation on the Fourth Gospel, Orbis Books, Maryknoll, 1979.
44   Op. cit., pp.121-2.

NOTES TO CHAPTER VI

Humanness in Christian Tradition
and Contemporary Debate

1   The New Testament: an Introduction, Harcourt Brace Jovanovich, New York, 1974, pp.287-88.
2   New Directions in New Testament Study, SCM, London, 1979, p.151.
3   To quote the title of Dietrich Ritschl's book, Memory and Hope: An Enquiry concerning the Presence of Christ, Macmillan, New York, 1967.
4   See P. Hebblethwaite, The New Inquisition? Schillebeeckx and Küng, Collins, London, 1980.
5   Op. cit., p.225. See his valuable account of biblical studies in the R.C. Church in ch.10: "The Apostolic Book and the Apostolic See." See also, R. E. Brown, "Rome and the Study of Scripture" in: J. M. Myers (ed.), Search the Scriptures, Brill, Leiden, 1969.
6   It is interesting to note that the constitution on the Sacred Liturgy takes up a position on regular worship on "the Lord's Day" not very different from that enjoined by the "Westminster Directory for the Publique Worship of God" (recently reprinted with an introduction by Ian Breward). While it does not forbid other "festival days, vulgarly called holy days," the Vatican document says, "The Lord's Day is therefore the first and greatest festival ... Other celebrations must not take precedence over it, unless they are truly of the

greatest importance, since it is the foundation and kernel of the whole liturgical year" (8).

7   B. O. McDermott, S.J., "Roman Catholic Christology: Two Recurring Themes," in: Theological Studies, vol.41 (1980), p.339. On Catholic biblical scholarship, R. E. Brown says, "In the first third of this century the torch of biblical criticism was kept lighted by Protestant scholars, and when after 1943 Catholics lighted their candles from it, they profited from the burnt fingers as well as the glowing insights of their Protestant confreres," (Biblical Reflections on Crises Facing the Church, Geoffrey Chapman, London, 1975, p.ix).

8   "The 'God of Jesus' and the 'Jesus of God'," in: Concilium, vol.3, no.10 (1974), p.113.

9   Patrick Henry, op. cit., p.23, summarizing Dunn's position. Only the most rigid fundamentalist would deny the diversity of the New Testament. A Festschrift for G. E. Ladd, a leading "conservative evangelical" American scholar, has the significant title: Unity and Diversity in New Testament Theology (ed. A. Guelich), Eerdmans, Grand Rapids, 1978, although it is difficult to see why this title was chosen. Ladd himself saw his book, A Theology of the New Testament, Eerdmans, Grand Rapids, 1974, as a "conservative evangelical attempt" to make a positive contribution to the discussion of unity and diversity of the New Testament to which little contribution had been hitherto made from that direction.

10   Ed. John Hick, SCM, London, 1975.

11   Michael Green (ed.), The Truth of God Incarnate, Hodder & Stoughton, London, 1975, and M. D. Goulder (ed.), Incarnation and Myth: The Debate Continued, SCM, London, 1979.

12   Op. cit., p.570.   13   Ibid., p.571.

14   Jesus, p.564, quoted Hebblethwaite, op. cit., p.135.

15   Schillebeeckx's written "Clarification," reprinted in Hebblethwaite, op. cit., p.134.

16   Right up to the time of delivery of the lectures in 1980 and after, my access to Kasper's criticism of Küng, as well as that of Rahner, was restricted to Bernard Sesboué's Bulletin, "Le dossier Hans Küng," in: Recherches de Science Religieuse, 67 (1979), pp. 567-598. These critical responses originally appeared in German in 1976 in: Diskussion über Hans Küng "Christ Sein", M. Grunewald, Mainz. I have still been unable to gain access to the original German, and have

had to rely on the translation into French: ed. J. R. Armogathe, Comment être Chrétien: la réponse de Hans Küng, Desclée de Brouwer, 1979.

17 See K. Rahner and W. Thüsing, A New Christology, Burns and Oates, London, 1980, Pt. I.

18 Küng, On Being a Christian, p. 442.

19 Kasper, "Etre chrétien sans tradition?," in: Armogathe, op. cit., p. 94.

20 Ibid.

21 Rahner, "Etre chrétien dans quelle église?," in: Armogathe, op. cit., p. 94.

22 Op. cit., p. 442.

23 I. H. Dalmais, "Divinisation - Patristique grecque"; G. Bardy, "Divinisation - Chez les pères latins."

24 Dalmais, op. cit., col. 1389.

25 Bardy, op. cit., col. 1398.

26 Jesus: God and Man, p. 39.

27 "Deification," in: P. Brooks (ed.), Christian Spirituality: Essays in Honour of Gordon Rupp, SCM, London, p. 50.

28 Harvey, vol. II, p. 314.

29 Adv. Haer., III, 19, 1.

30 Athanasius, De Incarnatione, 54; Ep. ad Adelphium, 14; Augustine, Sermo XIII de Tempore (Migne, P.L., 39, 1097-8.).

31 Sermo CLXXXXIV (P.L., 38, 1017); cf. Sermo CLXXXV, (P.L., 38, 999).

32 Sermo VI in Nativitate Domini, 5 (P.L., 54, 216).

33 See my Johannine Christology in the Early Church, pp. 137 ff.

34 The Dynamics of Salvation: A Study in Gregory of Nazianzus, (Patristic Monograph Series, No. 7), Philadelphia Patristic Foundation Ltd., 1979.

35 Ibid., p. 74.   36   Ibid., p. 119.

37 Or. 42, 17 (P.G., 36, 477C).

38 Winslow, op. cit., p. 186.

39 Ibid., 192 ff.   40   Ibid., 187 f.

41 It is interesting to note that Gregory actually uses the term "the humanity of God" (tôi anthrôpinôi tou theou) in Or. 45, 22 (P.G., 36, 6538); cf. Winslow, op. cit., p. 88.

42 Küng's christology may also be seen as a liberation theology, a cry for liberation from restrictive and oppressive ecclesiastical and theological structures which also give rise to injustice, inequality and denial of freedom.

INDEX OF BIBLICAL PASSAGES

Index of Biblical Passages

Index of Biblical Passages

INDEX OF AUTHORS

Index of Authors